Practice Book: Units 1–4

NATIONAL GEOGRAPHIC

Reach™ for Reading

COMMON CORE PROGRAM

NATIONAL GEOGRAPHIC LEARNING | CENGAGE Learning®

NATIONAL GEOGRAPHIC LEARNING | CENGAGE Learning

Acknowledgments
Grateful acknowledgment is given to the authors, artists, photographers, museums, publishers, and agents for permission to reprint copyrighted material. Every effort has been made to secure the appropriate permission. If any omissions have been made or if corrections are required, please contact the Publisher.

Cover Design and Art Direction: Visual Asylum

Cover illustration: Joel Sotelo

Illustration Credits: All PM illustrations by National Geographic Learning.

For product information and technology assistance, contact us at
Customer & Sales Support, 888-915-3276

For permission to use material from this text or product, submit all requests online at **www.cengage.com/permissions**
Further permissions questions can be emailed to
permissionrequest@cengage.com

National Geographic Learning | Cengage Learning
1 Lower Ragsdale Drive
Building 1, Suite 200
Monterey, CA 93940

Cengage Learning is a leading provider of customized learning solutions with office locations around the globe, including Singapore, the United Kingdom, Australia, Mexico, Brazil, and Japan. Locate your local office at **www.cengage.com/global**.

Cengage Learning products are represented in Canada by Nelson Education, Ltd.

Visit National Geographic Learning online at **NGL.Cengage.com**
Visit our corporate website a **www.cengage.com**

Printed in the USA.
Sheridan, KY, A CJK Group Company

ISBN: 978-13054-98990 (Practice Book)

ISBN: 978-13056-58691 (Practice Masters)

Teachers are authorized to reproduce the practice masters in this book in limited quantity and solely for use in their own classrooms.

Printed in the United States of America

21 22 23 24

16 15

Contents

Unit 1: My Family

Unit 2: Shoot for the Sun

Unit 3: To Your Front Door

Unit 4: Growing and Changing

Name ____________________ Date __________

Phonics

Letter and Sound Mm

Mm

Write the missing letter. Color each item named in the sentence.

1.

mop

2.

an

3.

ask

4.

ouse

5.

ilk

6.

itt

7.

oon

8.
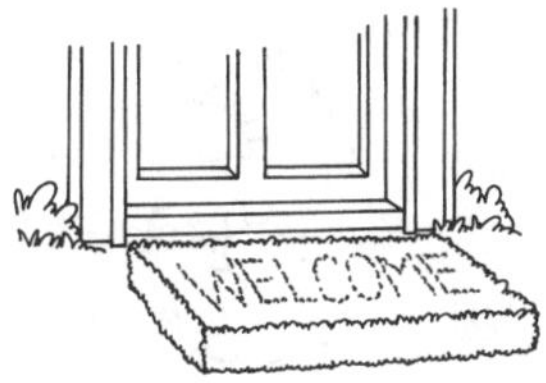

at

9.
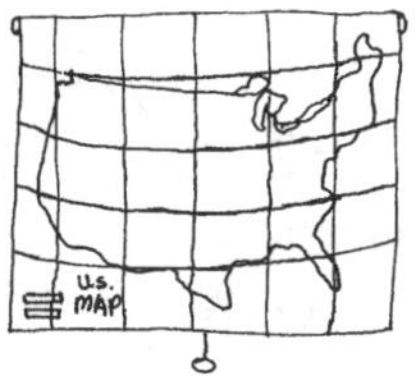

ap

Read It Together Find the man and the mat.

Name ______________________ Date ____________

Phonics

Letter and Sound Ss

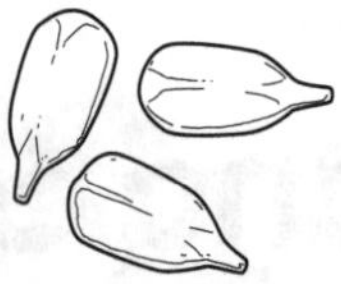

Ss

Write the missing letter. Color each item named in the sentence.

1. 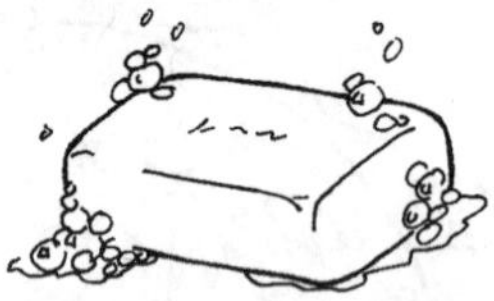 soap	**2.**  ilk	**3.**  un
4. 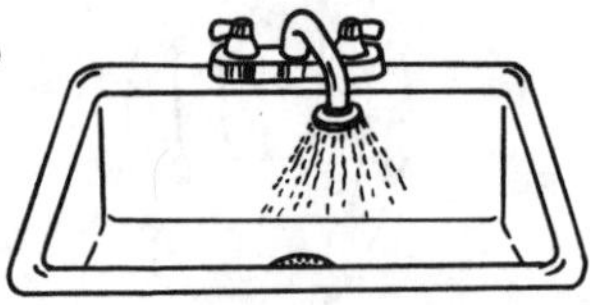 ink	**5.** 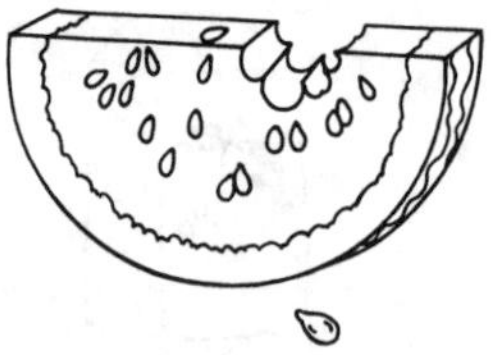 eed	**6.** 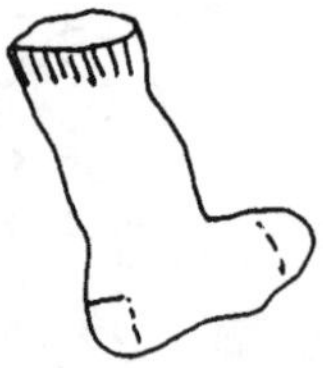 ock
7.  eal	**8.** 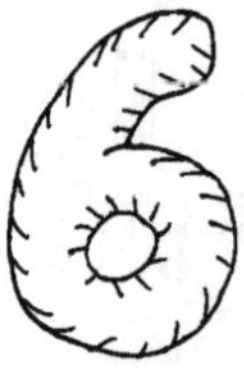 ix	**9.**  even

Read It Together Find the sun and the six.

Name ______________________ Date ____________

Phonics

Letter and Sound Hh

Hh

Write the missing letter. Color each item named in the sentence.

1. 

hat

2. 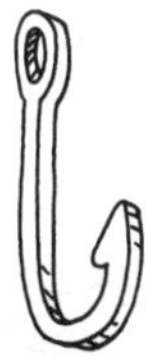

ook

3. 

un

4. 

ask

5. 

an

6. 

ose

7. 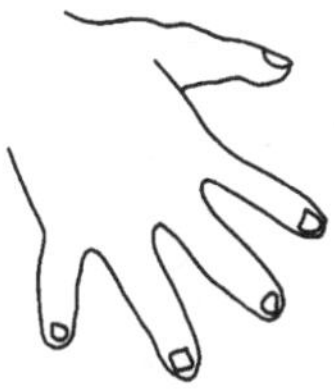

and

8. 

ouse

9. 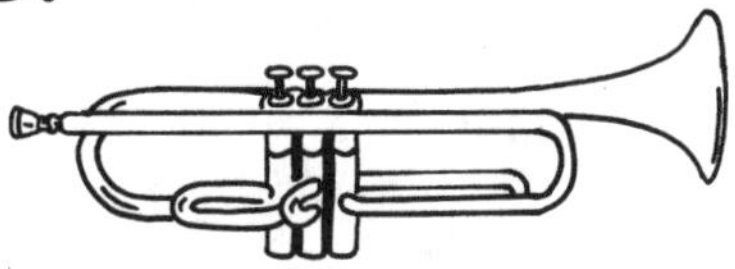

orn

Read It Together Find the hat and the hand.

Name ______________________ Date ____________

Phonics

Letter and Sound Tt

Tt

Write the missing letter. Color each item named in the sentence.

1. 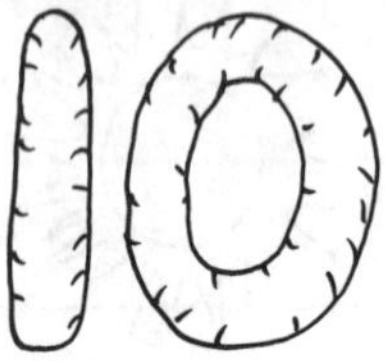 ten

2.  itt

3.  ape

4. 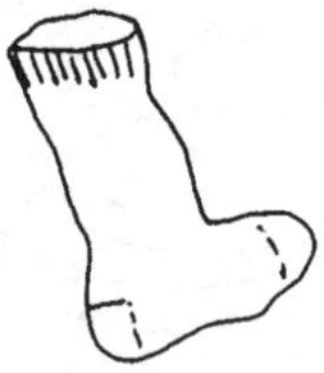 ock

5.  ub

6.  ire

7.  orse

8.  op

9. 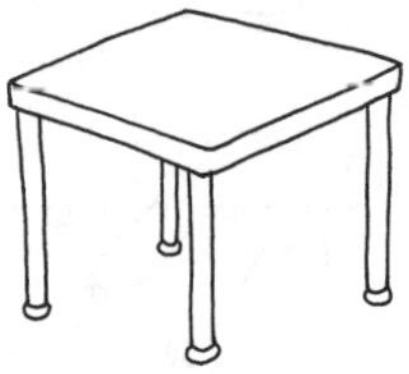 able

Read It Together Find the ten and the tub.

Name ____________________ Date ____________

Handwriting

High Frequency Words

Trace each word two times and then write it.

find find find

has has has

have have have

his his his

mother mother mother

too too too

Name ______________________ Date ____________

Cut out the pictures and the book. Fold the book on the solid lines. Paste an *m* picture on each page and write its name. Read the sentence and color what it names.

Read It Together

Find the man.

My M m Book

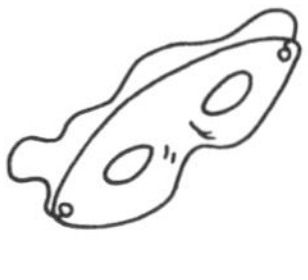

Name ______________________ Date ____________

Cut out the pictures and the book. Fold the book on the solid lines. Paste an *s* picture on each page and write its name. Read the sentence and color what it names.

Read It Together

Find the Sun.

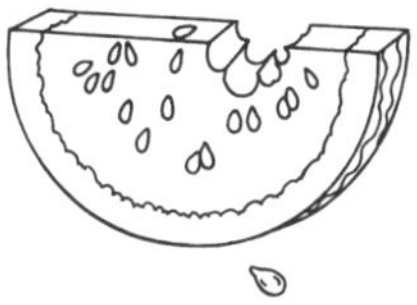

My S s Book

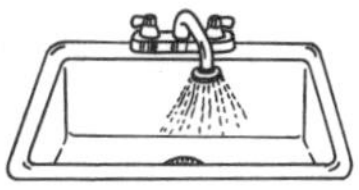

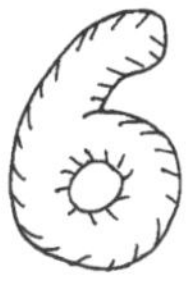

Name ______________________________ Date ____________

Cut out the pictures and the book. Fold the book on the solid lines. Paste an *h* picture on each page and write its name. Read the sentence and color what it names.

Read It Together

Find the hat.

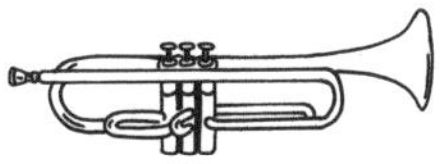

My H h Book

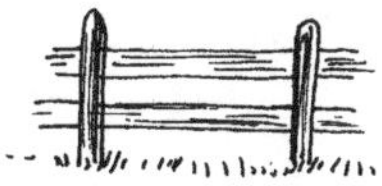

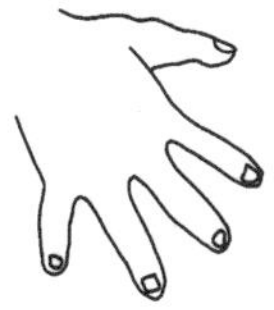

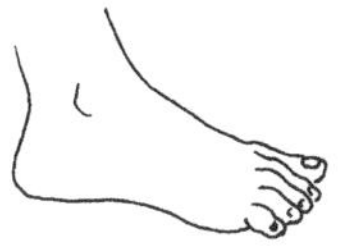

Name ______________________ Date ______________

Cut out the pictures and the book. Fold the book on the solid lines. Paste a *t* picture on each page and write its name. Read the sentence and color what it names.

Read It Together

Find the tub.

My T t Book

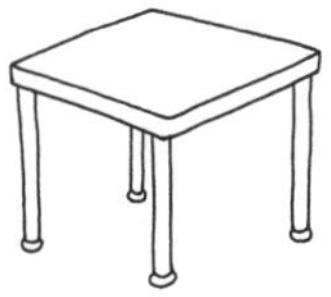

Spelling & Word Work

High Frequency Word Cards

a	find
am	has
I	have
is	his
like	mother
my	too

Name ____________________ Date __________

Idea Web

Organize Ideas

Write about what your family does together.

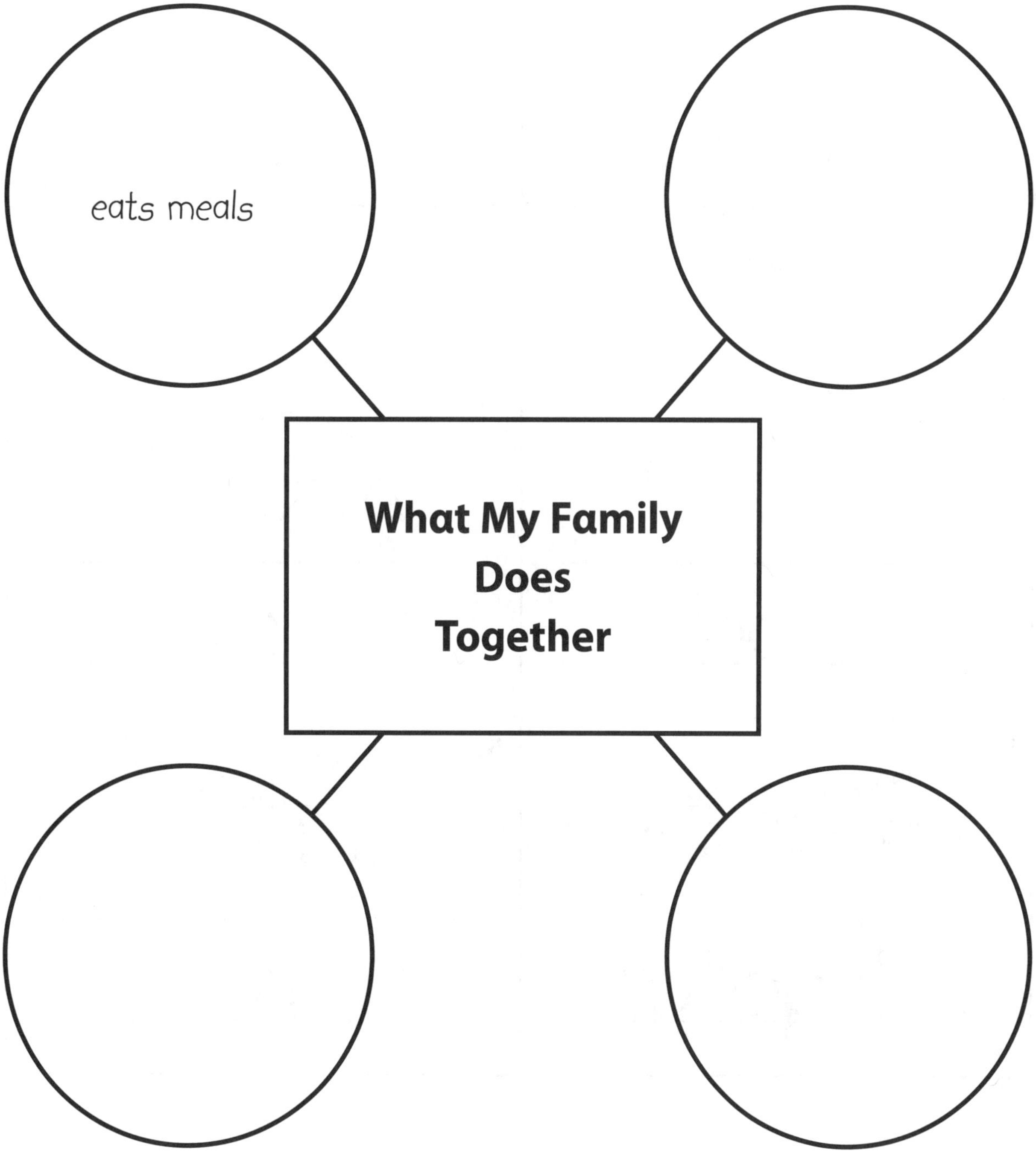

Name ______________________ Date ____________

Phonics

Letter and Sound Aa

Aa

Write the missing letter. Color the item named in the sentence.

1.  apple	2.  op
3.  x	4.  ox
5. 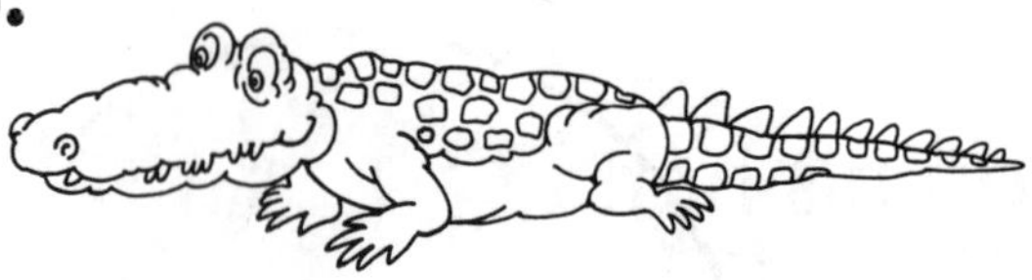 lligator	6. 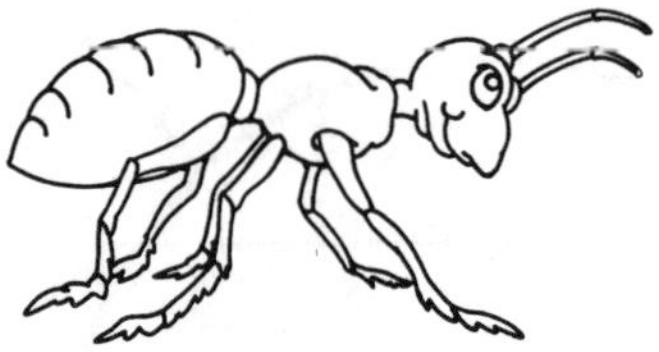 nt

Read It Together Find the ax.

Name ______________________ Date ____________

High Frequency Words

Find a Hat

Write a word from the box to complete each sentence.

High Frequency Words
find
has
have
his
mother
too

1. Sam ____________ a hat.

2. ____________ hat is on the mat.

3. His ____________ sat on his hat!

4. I have a hat, ____________.

5. ____________ my hat!

Name ______________________ Date ____________

Grammar: Nouns

Use Nouns

1. Play Tic Tac Toe. Point to a square.
2. Say the word. Tell whether it names one or more than one person, place, or thing.
3. Use the word in a sentence.
4. If you choose the middle square, name your own noun. Complete steps 2 and 3.
5. Place your game marker in the square.

 **child**	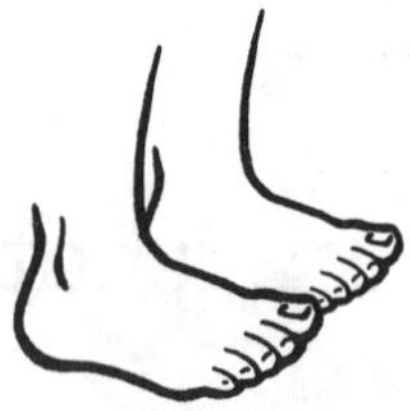 **feet**	 **woman**
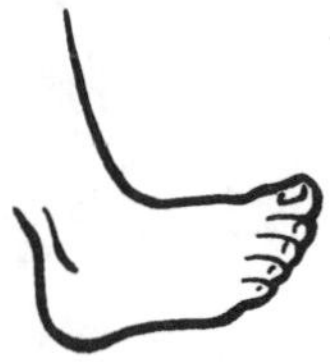 **foot**	**Draw a noun. Name it.**	 **men**
 **man**	 **women**	 **children**

Name ____________________ Date ____________

Cut out the pictures and the book. Fold the book on the solid lines. Paste an *a* picture on each page and write its name. Read the sentence and color what it names.

Read It Together

Find the ant.

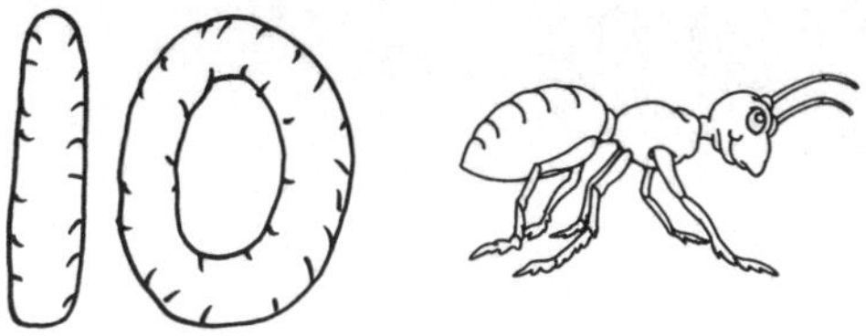

My A a Book

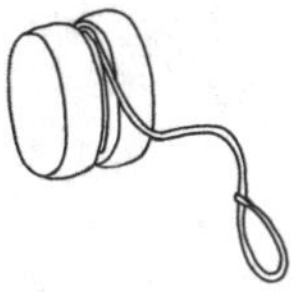

Name ______________________ Date ____________

Grammar and Writing

Write Nouns

Singular Nouns	Plural Nouns
child	children
brother	brothers
house	houses

Read each sentence. Find a word from the word bank that completes the sentence. Write the word in the sentence.

1. My mom and dad are my (parent/parents).

2. They have two (child/children).

3. I have one (brother/brothers).

4. We live in a (house/houses).

5. We play many (game/games).

6. I love my (family/families).

Name ______________________ Date ____________

Vocabulary

Yes or No?

1. Listen to the questions. Write the Key Word where it belongs in each sentence.
2. Listen to the questions again.
3. Check Yes or No for each question.

	Yes	No
1. Is breakfast a meal?	✓	☐
2. Is a teacher a ______________?	☐	☐
3. Can an apartment be a ______________?	☐	☐
4. Is New Year's Day a ______________?	☐	☐
5. Can you ______________ a birthday?	☐	☐
6. Is a group of students a ______________?	☐	☐

Name ______________________ Date ____________

Idea Web

Families in Many Cultures

Write about what families do together.

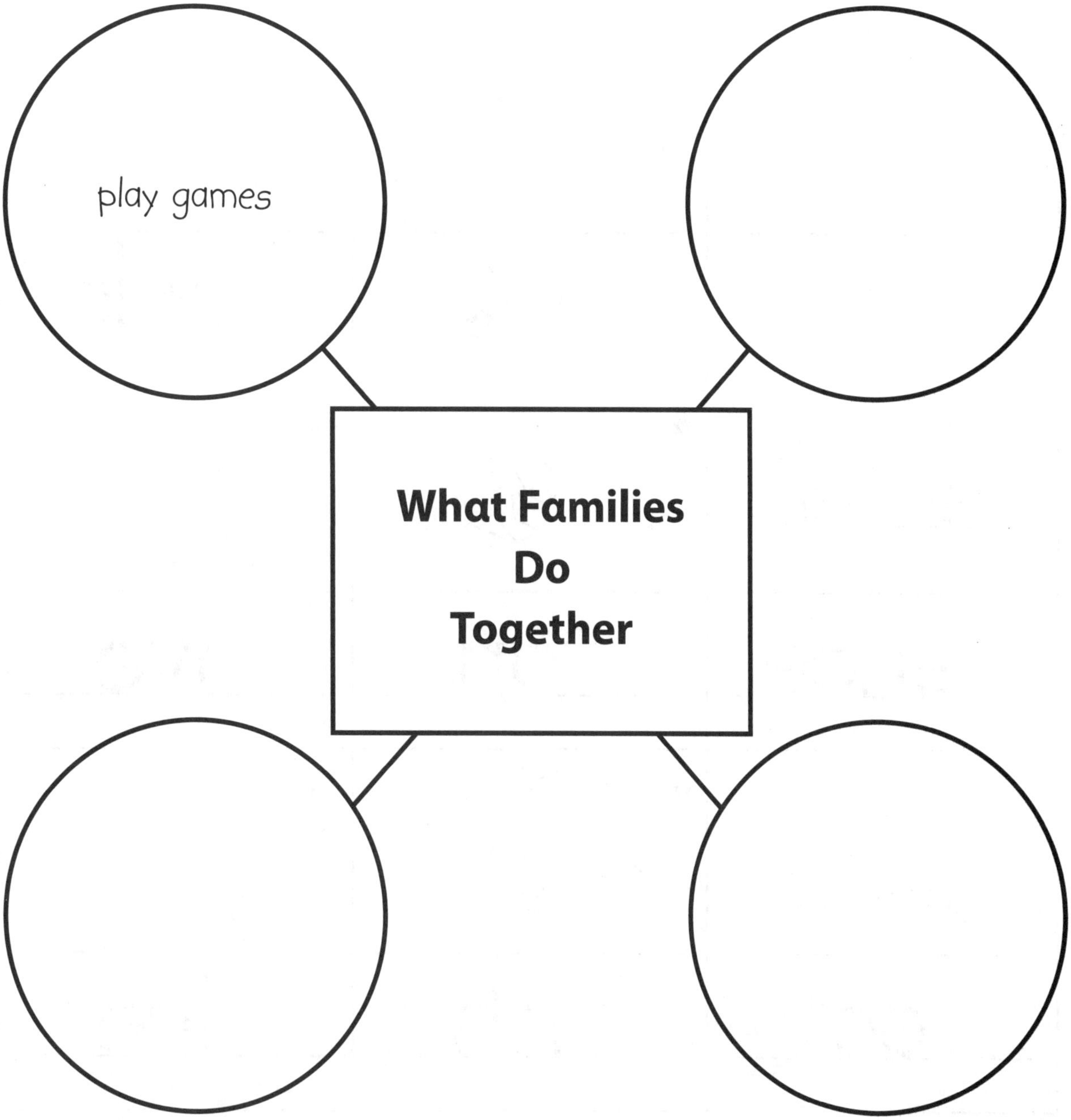

Read It Together Take turns with a partner. Tell what you learned about families in "Families in Many Cultures."

Name ______________________ Date ____________

Phonics

Letter and Sound Ff

Ff

Write the missing letter. Color each item named in the sentence.

1.  fox	**2.** 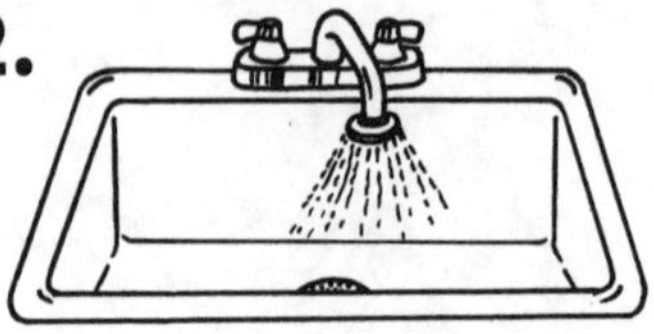 ink	**3.**  ork
4. 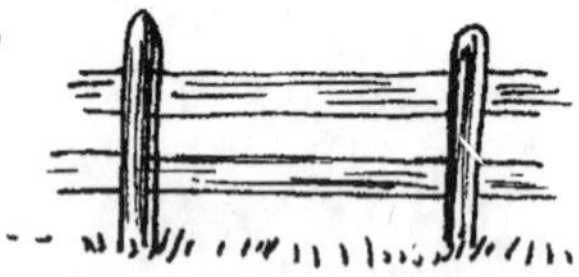 ence	**5.**  an	**6.**  ive
7. 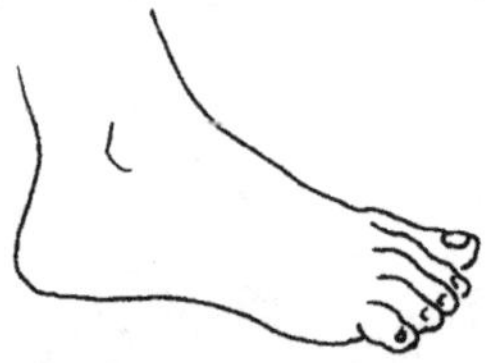 oot	**8.**  ish	**9.**  ire

Read It Together Find the fan and the fox.

Name ____________________ Date __________

Phonics

Letter and Sound Nn

Nn

Write the missing letter. Color each item named in the sentence.

1.  nut	**2.** 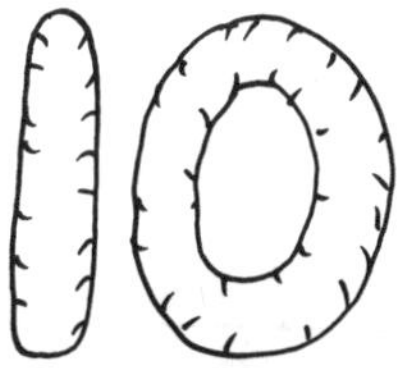 en	**3.** 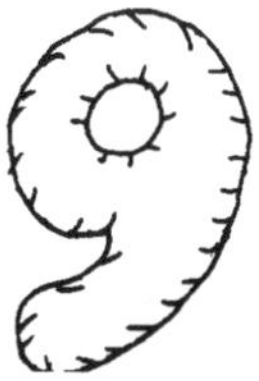 ine
4.  op	**5.** 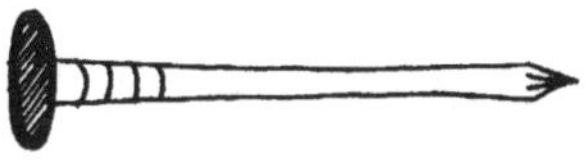 ail	**6.** 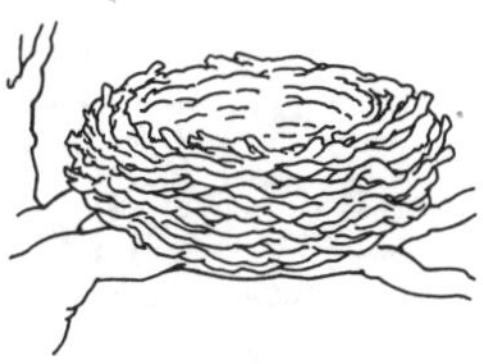 est
7. 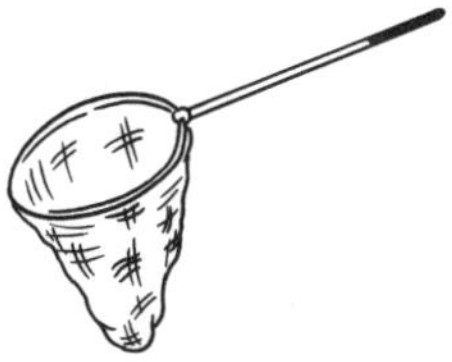 et	**8.**  ose	**9.**  ox

Read It Together Find a nut and a net.

Name ______________________________ Date ______________

Phonics

Letter and Sound Ll

Ll

Write the missing letter. Color each item named in the sentence.

1.  leg	**2.**  ub	**3.**  emon
4. 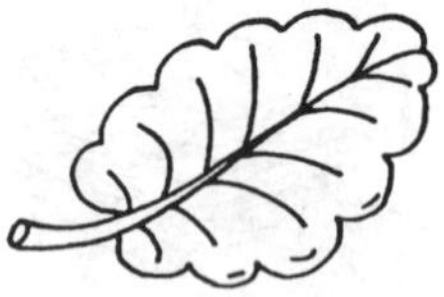 eaf	**5.** 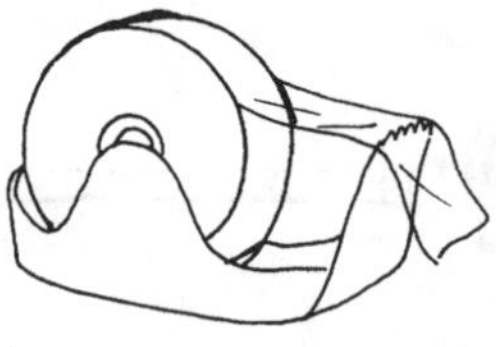 ape	**6.**  amb
7.  orn	**8.**  og	**9.**  amp

Read It Together Find the leg and the log.

Name ______________________ Date __________

Phonics

Letter and Sound Pp

Pp

Write the missing letter. Color each item named in the sentence.

1.  pen	2.  __at	3. 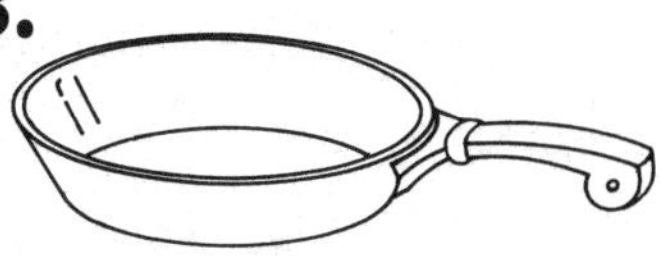 __an
4.  __ear	5. 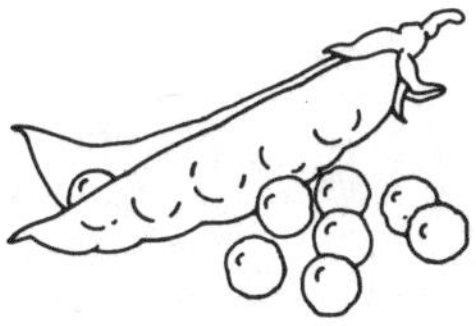 __eas	6.  __un
7.  __ire	8. 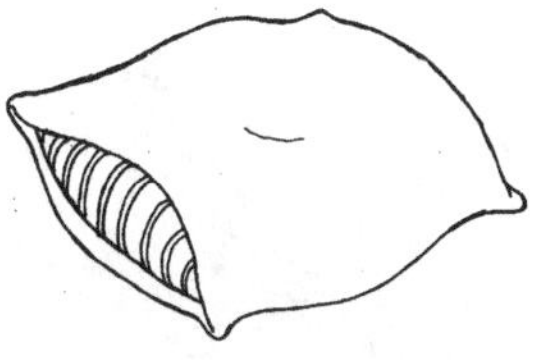 __illow	9. 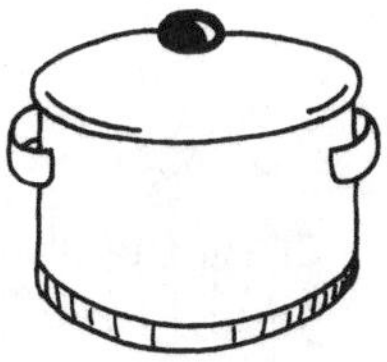 __ot

Read It Together Find the pan and the pot.

Name ____________________ Date ____________

Phonics

Letter and Sound Cc

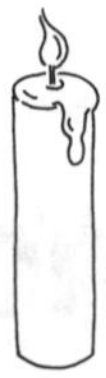

Cc

Write the missing letter. Color each item named in the sentence.

1.  cat	**2.**  _up	**3.** 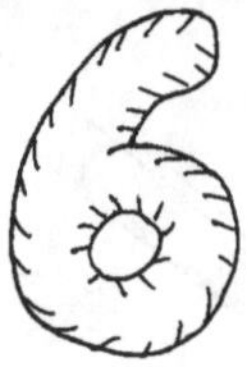 _ix
4.  _an	**5.** 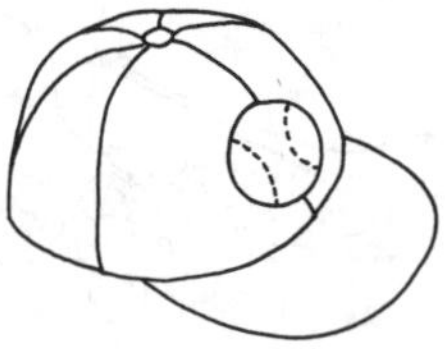 _ap	**6.** 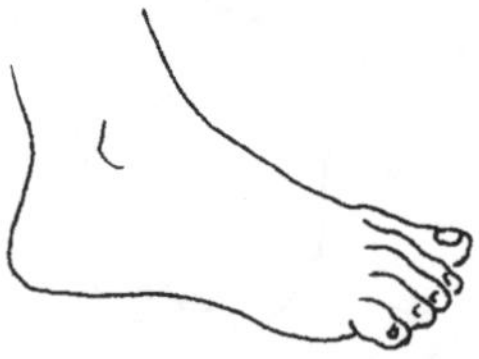 _oot
7.  _ouse	**8.**  _orn	**9.**  _ow

Read It Together Find the cat and the cap.

Name ______________________ Date ____________

Grammar

Choose A or An

holiday	brother	egg
apple	friend	grandfather
sister	home	uncle
bed	orange	table
aunt	parent	meal
grandmother	banana	sister

Name ______________________________ Date ______________

Handwriting

High Frequency Words

Trace each word two times and then write it.

do do do

then then then

what what what

with with with

you you you

your your your

Name ______________________ Date ____________

Cut out the pictures and the book. Fold the book on the solid lines. Paste an *f* picture on each page and write its name. Read the sentence and color what it names.

Read It Together

Find the fan.

My F f Book

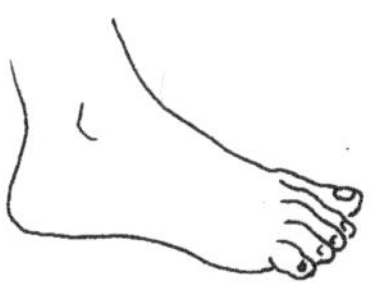

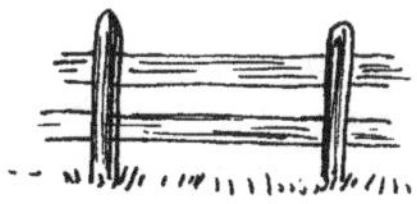

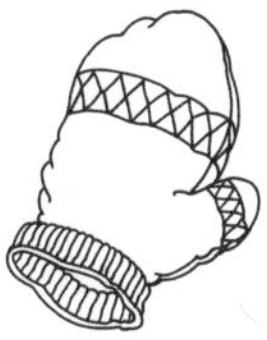

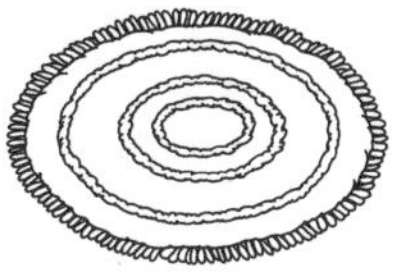

Name ______________________ Date ____________

Cut out the pictures and the book. Fold the book on the solid lines. Paste an *n* picture on each page and write its name. Read the sentence and color what it names.

Read It Together

Find the nap.

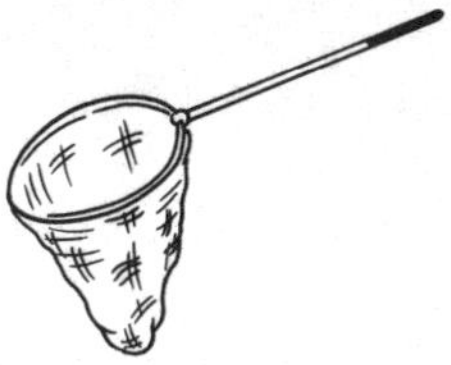

My N n Book

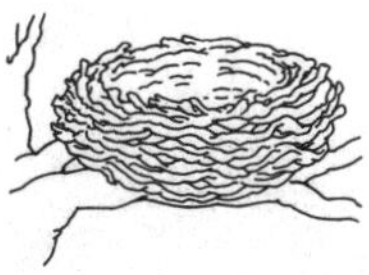

Name ______________________ Date ______________

Cut out the pictures and the book. Fold the book on the solid lines. Paste an *l* picture on each page and write its name. Read the sentence and color what it names.

Read It Together

Find the lamp.

My L l Book

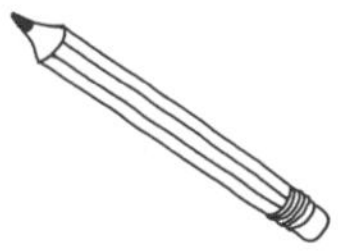

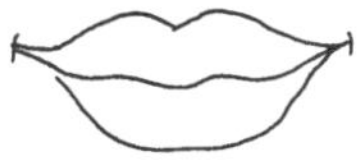

Name ______________________ Date ____________

Cut out the pictures and the book. Fold the book on the solid lines. Paste a *p* picture on each page and write its name. Read the sentence and color what it names.

Read It Together

Find the pan.

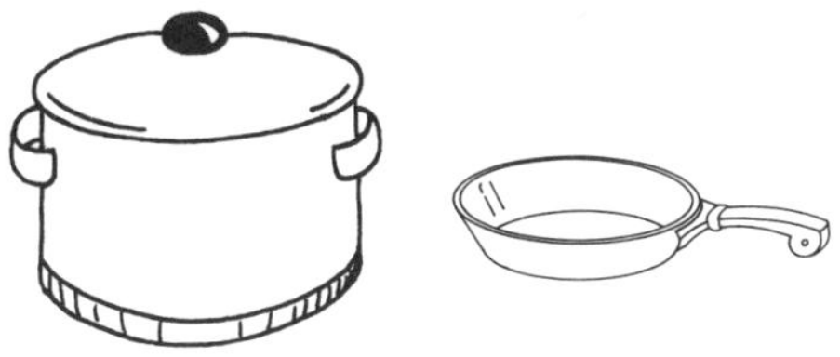

My P p Book

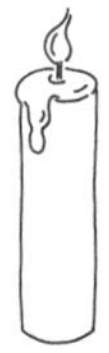

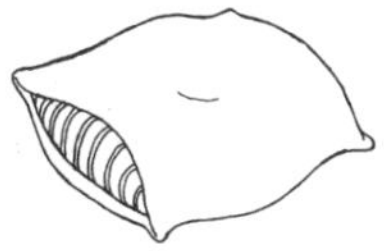

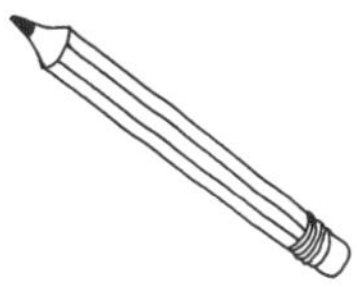
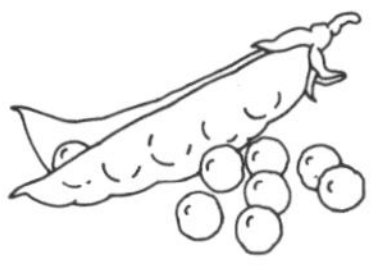

Name ______________________ Date ____________

Cut out the pictures and the book. Fold the book on the solid lines. Paste a *c* picture on each page and write its name. Read the sentence and color what it names.

Read It Together

Find the can.

My C c Book

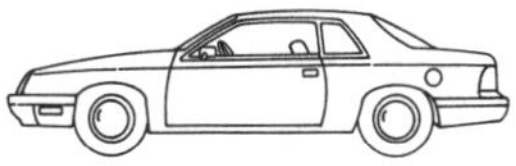

High Frequency Word Cards

and	do
little	then
that	what
the	with
this	you
on	your

Name ______________________ Date ______________

T-Chart

Compare Authors' Purposes

Compare "Families in Many Cultures" and "The World Is Your Family."

"Families in Many Cultures"	"The World Is Your Family"
to show families in different places	

Read It Together Take turns with a partner. Tell how the authors' purposes are different.

Name ____________________ Date ____________

Phonics

Letter and Sound Ii

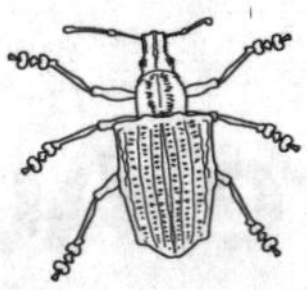

Ii

Write the missing letter. Color each item named in the sentence.

1.

insect

2.

all

3.

pple

4.

gloo

5.

ll

6.

even

Read It Together Find the insect and the igloo.

Name ______________________ Date ____________

High Frequency Words

Find Nat!

Write a word from the box to complete each sentence.

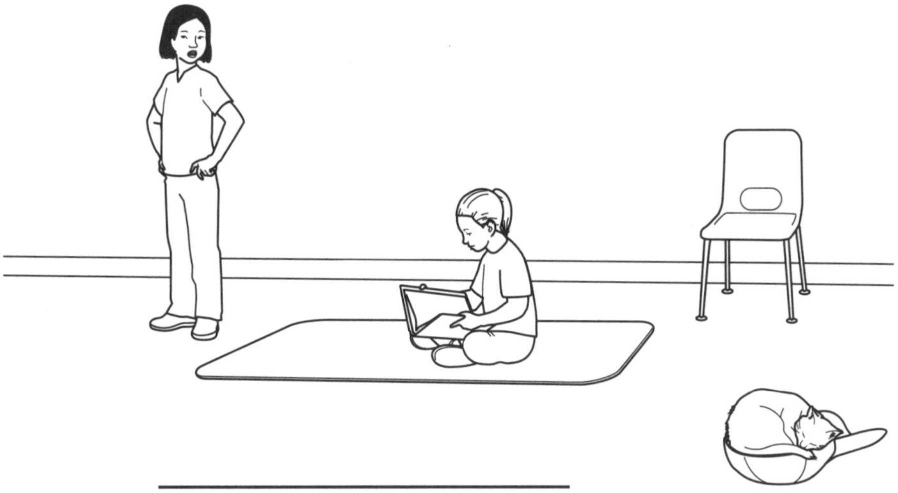

High Frequency **Words**
do
then
what
with
you
your

1. Can ______________ find Nat the cat?

2. Is Nat on the mat ______________ Pam?

3. ______________ is that in the cap?

4. Nat, ______________ you like to nap?

5. ______________ you can nap in your cap!

Name ______________________ Date ____________

Cut out the pictures and the book. Fold the book on the solid lines. Paste an *i* picture on each page and write its name. Draw a picture to go with the sentence.

Read It Together

Draw a wig on a pig.

My I i Book

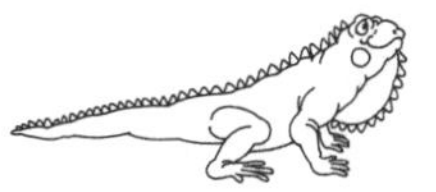

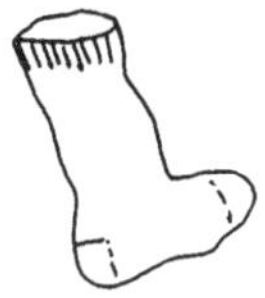

Name ______________________ Date ____________

Grammar and Writing

Write Articles and Plural Nouns

1. Read the story.

2. Circle the correct articles.

3. Fill in the blanks with plural nouns. Add *-s* or *-es*.

It takes a lot of work to make (a/the) garden! First, we cleaned up (a/the) yard. Then we moved two ______________ (bench) near the garden. Next, we bought some seeds. I got ______________ (bean) and ______________ (sunflower). I also got (a/an) apple seed. We planted (a/the) seeds. We watered them with (a/an) hose. I can't wait to eat from (a/the) garden!

Name ______________________ Date ____________

Vocabulary

Name It!

Grammar Rules Plural Nouns

- Add *s* to most nouns to show more than one.

  meal → meal<u>s</u>

- Add *es* to nouns that end with *ss*, *x*, *ch*, and *sh* to show more than one.

  lunch → lunch<u>es</u>

glass | sandwich | teacher | mother

meal

BEGIN

lunch

park

box

END

brother | dish | class | bowl

1. Play with a partner.
2. Use a small object for a game piece.
3. Flip a coin.

    = Move 1 space.

    = Move 2 spaces.
4. Say the singular noun.
5. Write the plural form on another sheet of paper.
6. The first one to the END wins!

Name ______________________ Date ____________

Phonics

Letter and Sound Gg

Gg

Write the missing letter. Color each item named in the sentence.

1.

girl

2.

___up

3.

___ift

4.

___at

5.

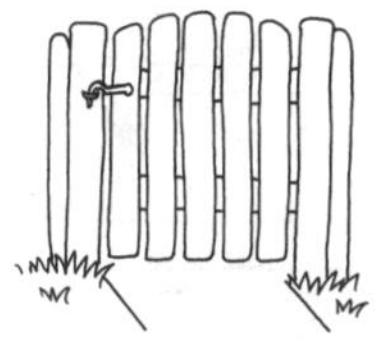

___ate

6.

___uitar

7.

___oat

8.

___ion

9.

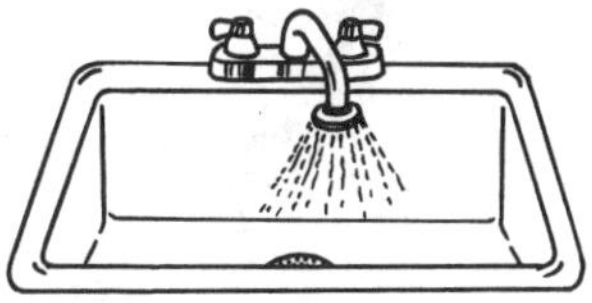

___ink

Read It Together Find the gate and the goat.

Name ______________________ Date ____________

Phonics

Letter and Sound Dd  Dd

Write the missing letter. Color each item named in the sentence.

1.  dog	**2.** 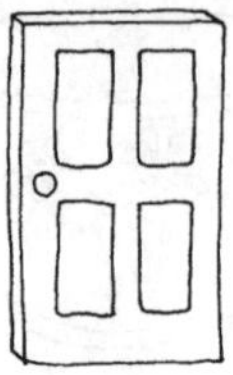 oor	**3.** 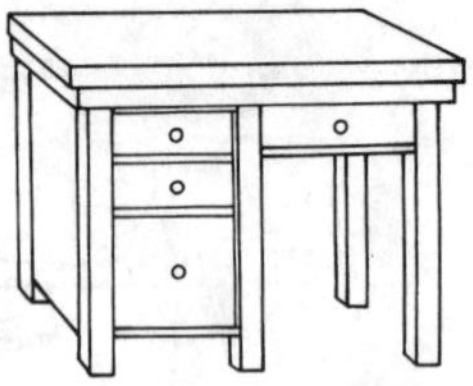 esk
4.  ime	**5.** 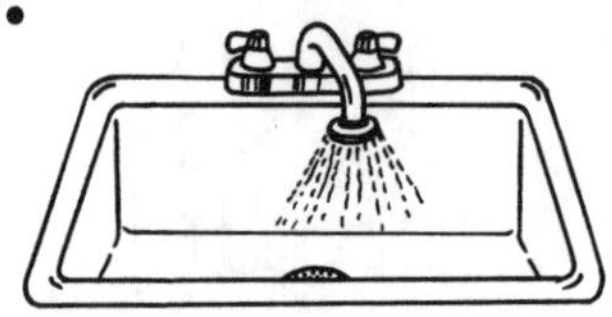 ink	**6.**  uck
7.  irl	**8.**  oll	**9.**  eer

Read It Together Find the duck and the door.

Name ______________________ Date ____________

Phonics

Letter and Sound Vv  Vv

Write the missing letter. Color each item named in the sentence.

1.

van

2.

uck

3.

eaf

4.
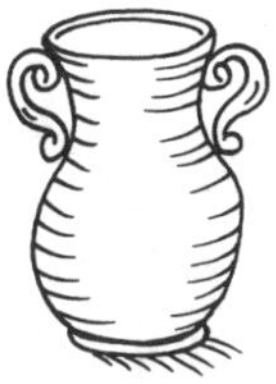

ase

5.

ing

6.

og

7.

at

8.
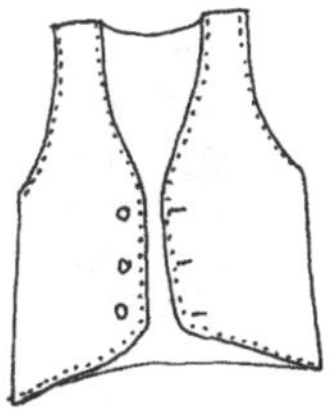

est

9.
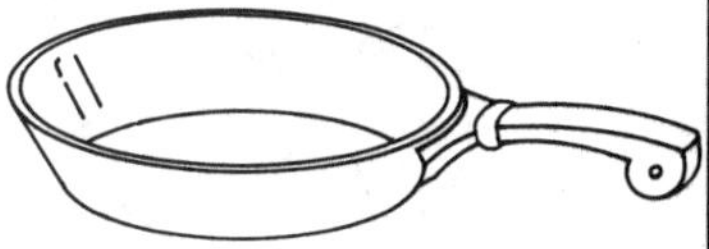

an

Read It Together Find the vest and the vase.

Name ____________________ Date __________

Phonics

Letter and Sound Rr

Rr

Write the missing letter. Color each item named in the sentence.

1.

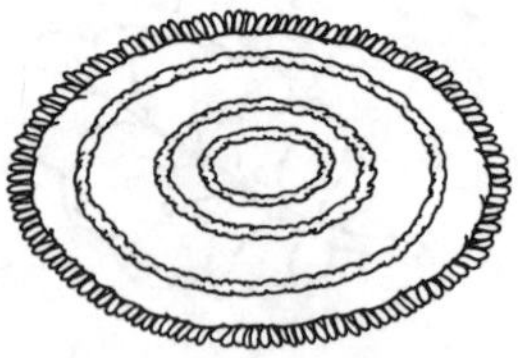

rug

2.

___en

3.

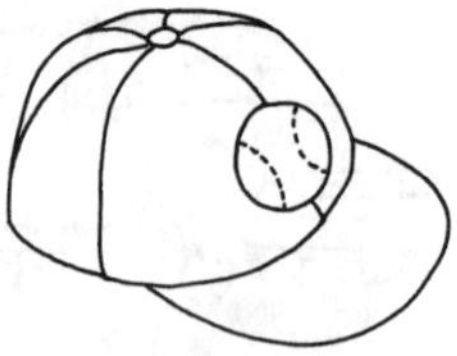

___ap

4.

___oad

5.

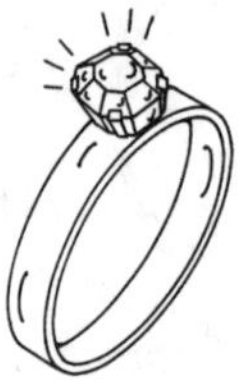

___ing

6.

___ake

7.

___ish

8.

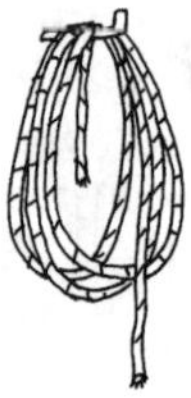

___ope

9.

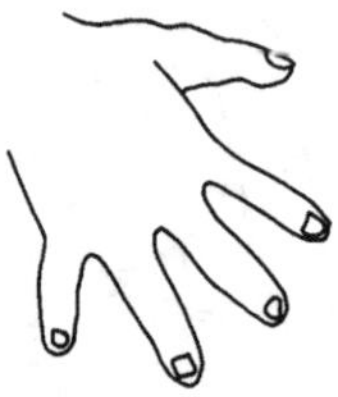

___and

Read It Together Find the rake and the rug.

Name ______________________ Date ____________

Handwriting

High Frequency Words

Trace each word two times and then write it.

get get get

help help help

of of of

put put put

we we we

work work work

Name ______________________ Date ____________

Cut out the pictures and the book. Fold the book on the solid lines. Paste a *g* picture on each page and write its name. Read the sentence and do what it says.

Read It Together

Put an X on the cat.

My G g Book

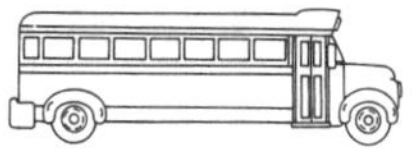

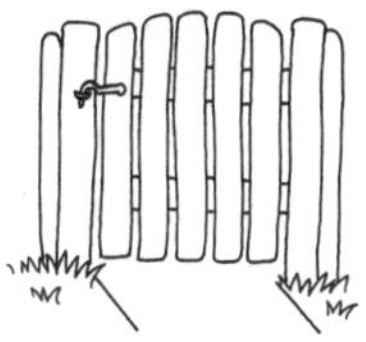

Name ______________________ Date ____________

Cut out the pictures and the book. Fold the book on the solid lines. Paste a *d* picture on each page and write its name. Read the sentence and color what it names.

Read It Together

Find the dog.

My D d Book

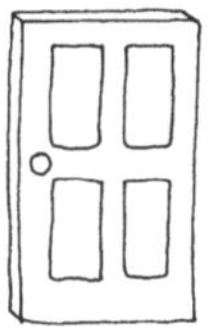

Name ______________________________ Date ______________

Cut out the pictures and the book. Fold the book on the solid lines. Paste a *v* picture on each page and write its name. Read the sentence and color what it names.

Read It Together

Find the van.

My V v Book

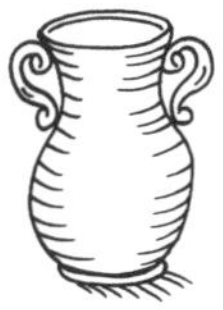

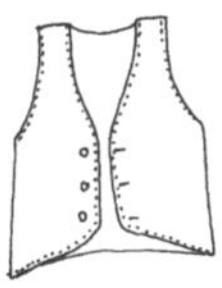

Name ______________________ Date ____________

Cut out the pictures and the book. Fold the book on the solid lines. Paste an *r* picture on each page and write its name. Read the sentence and do what it says.

Read It Together

Put an X on the fan.

My R r Book

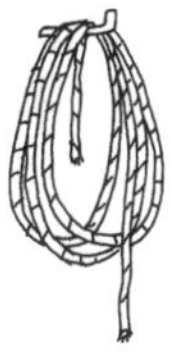

Spelling & Word Work

High Frequency Word Cards

her	get
him	help
too	of
with	put
you	we
your	work

Name ______________________ Date ____________

Setting Chart

Identify Setting

Write the setting of a family story you know at the top of the left column. Write about the setting below. Draw a picture of the setting in the right column.

Setting: ____________	Picture of the Place

Name ______________________ Date ______________

Phonics

Letter and Sound Oo

Oo

Write the missing letter. Put a dot by the item named.

1.

ostrich

2.

_x

3.

_tter

4.

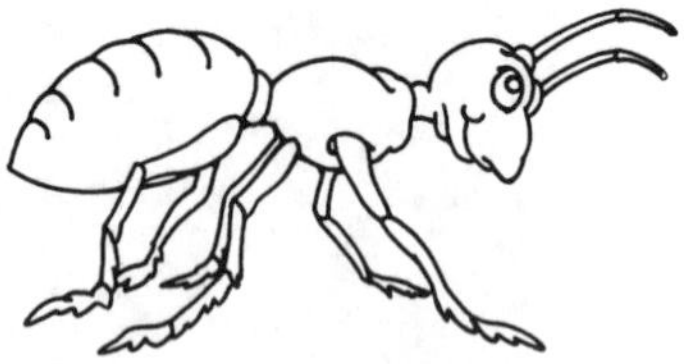

_nt

5.

_ish

6.

_live

Read It Together Put a big dot by the ox.

Name ______________________ Date __________

High Frequency Words

A Big Help

Write a word from the box to complete each sentence.

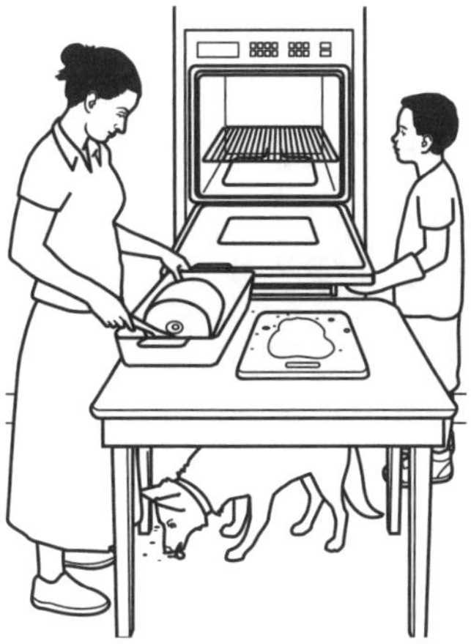

High Frequency Words
get
help
of
put
we
work

1. I ______________ with Mom.

2. We ______________ a ham.

3. We ______________ the ham in a pan.

4. My dog can ______________, too.

5. My dog can do a lot ______________ work!

Name ______________________ Date ____________

Grammar: Common and Proper Nouns

Use Proper Nouns

1. Point to a picture.
2. Use a common noun to name the place.
3. Then use a proper noun to name the place. Make up a name or use the name of a real place.
4. Say your sentences to your partner.

Name ______________________ Date __________

Cut out the pictures and the book. Fold the book on the solid lines. Paste an *o* picture on each page and write its name. Read the sentence and do what it says.

Read It Together

Put an X on the cap.

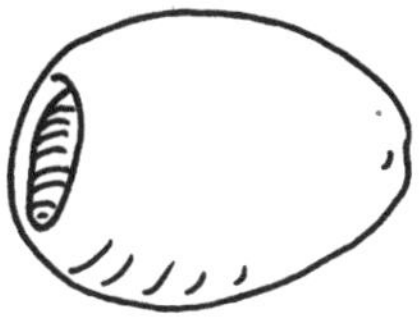
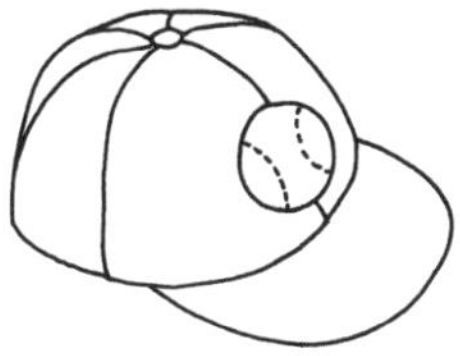

My O o Book

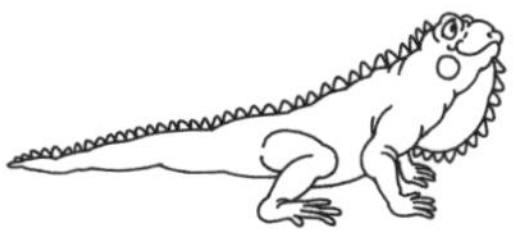

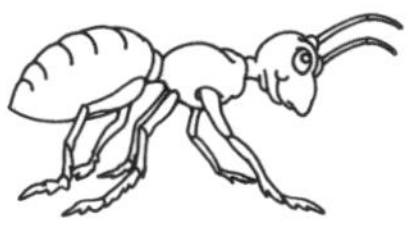
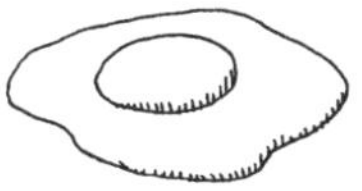

Name ______________________ Date ____________

Phonics

Final -s

Circle the word that completes each sentence and write it.

hat **hats**

1. Bob has lots of ______________ .

has **his**

2. Bob ______________ a dog, too.

has **is**

3. Rags ______________ his dog.

get **gets**

4. Bob ______________ Rags a hat.

his **is**

5. Rags likes ______________ hat.

Name ______________________________ Date ______________

Grammar and Writing

Write Common and Proper Nouns

state	dog	Shell Beach	brother	Miami	Ashley

Look at each pair of sentences. Look at the underlined word in the first sentence. Draw a line to the common or proper noun that completes the second sentence.

1. This is my sister. Her name is ________ .	brother
2. This is James. He is my ________ .	Ashley
3. We live in a big city. It is called ________ .	Miami
4. Miami is in Florida. Our ________ is in the south.	state
5. We swim at the beach. We often go to ________ .	dog
6. Buddy splashes in the waves with us. Buddy is our ________ .	Shell Beach

Name ______________________________ Date ______________

Vocabulary

Family Trip Bingo

1. Write one Key Word in each suitcase.
2. Listen to the clues. Place a marker on the Key Word.
3. Say "Bingo" when you have four markers in a row.

Name ______________________________ Date ______________

Setting Chart

Papá and Me

List the places that Papá and his son went. Then list words that tell what the places are like.

Places	What the Places are Like
• home	• fun
•	•
•	•
•	•

Take turns with a partner. Use your setting chart to give information about the story.

Name ____________________ Date ____________

Phonics

Letter and Sound Bb  Bb

Write the missing letter. Color the item named in the sentence.

1.  bat	**2.** 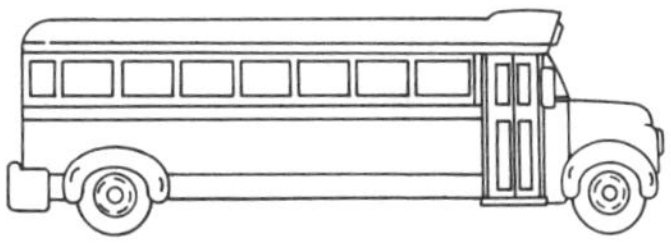 us	**3.**  un
4.  an	**5.**  ed	**6.**  an
7.  ee	**8.**  ird	**9.**  oy

Read It Together Find the bed.

Name ______________________ Date ____________

Phonics

Letter and Sound Ww 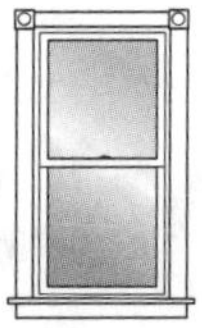 Ww

Write the missing letter. Color each item named in the sentence.

1. 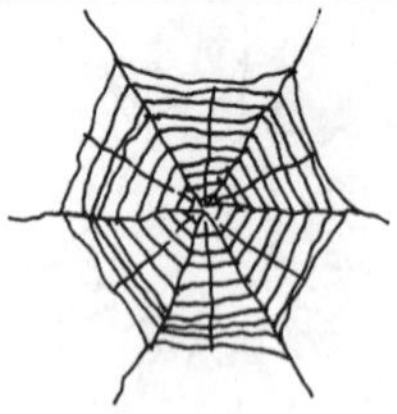 web	**2.** 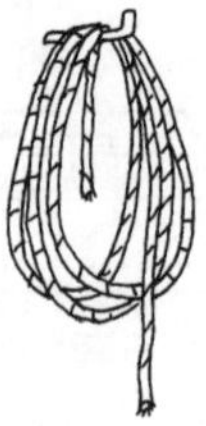 _ope	**3.**  _ave
4. 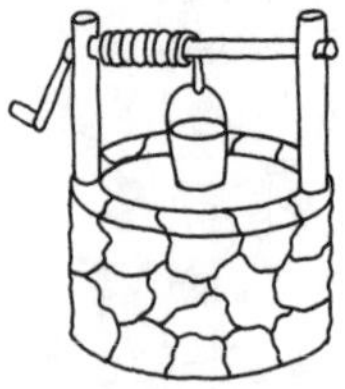 _ell	**5.**  _ee	**6.**  _ing
7.  _ig	**8.**  _ook	**9.**  _an

Read It Together Find the wing and the well.

Name ______________________ Date ____________

Phonics

Letter and Sound Jj

Jj

Write the missing letter. Put a dot on the item named.

1. 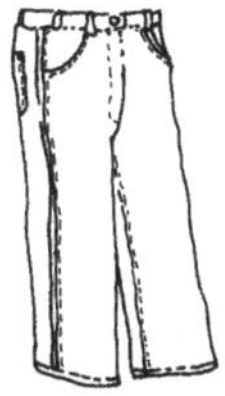 jeans	**2.**  acket	**3.**  og
4.  eer	**5.**  et	**6.**  eal
7.  ion	**8.**  ar	**9.** 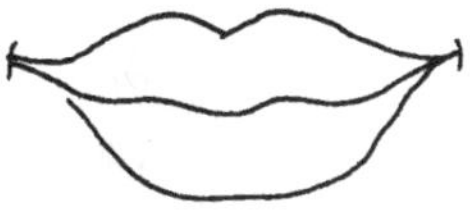 ips

Read It Together Put a dot on the jet.

Name ______________________ Date ______________

Phonics

Letter and Sound Zz

Zz

Write the missing letter. Color each item named in the sentence.

1.

tub

2.

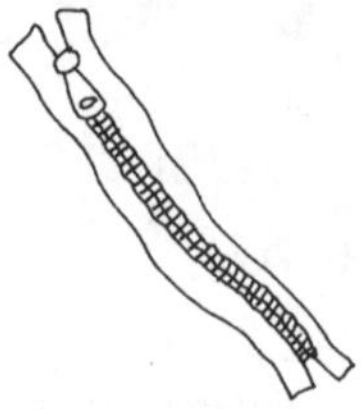

ipper

3.

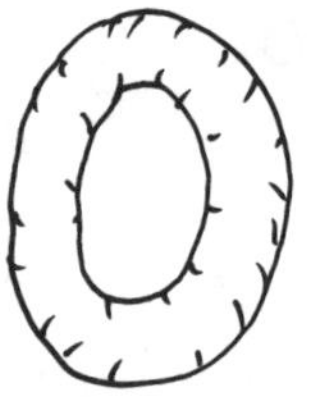

ero

4.

ase

5.

oo

6.

ock

Read It Together Find the zoo and the zipper.

Name ______________________ Date ____________

Grammar: Proper Nouns

Find Proper Nouns

1. Take turns with a partner.
2. Read the word in the box.
3. If it is a proper noun, write it on a piece of paper with a capital letter.
4. If it is a common noun, don't write anything.
5. Color all the boxes with a proper noun to get Fluffy to the vet.

fluffy	nebraska	monday
home	trip	amy
idea	carlos	june
oak street	friday	share
october	group	visit
wisconsin	sunday	doctor dan

Name ______________________ Date ____________

Handwriting

High Frequency Words

Trace each word two times and then write it.

day day day

from from from

good good good

she she she

us us us

very very very

Name ______________________ Date ____________

Cut out the pictures and the book. Fold the book on the solid lines. Paste a *b* picture on each page and write its name. Read the sentence and color what it names.

Read It Together

Find the bat.

My B b Book

Name ______________________________ Date ______________

Cut out the pictures and the book. Fold the book on the solid lines. Paste a *w* picture on each page and write its name. Read the sentence and color what it names.

Read It Together

Find the wave.

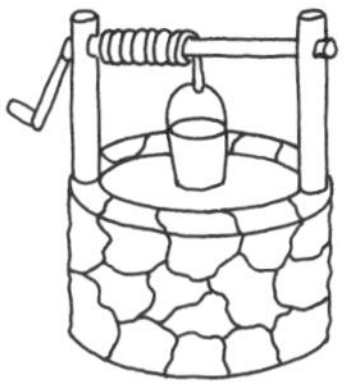

My W w Book

____

____

____

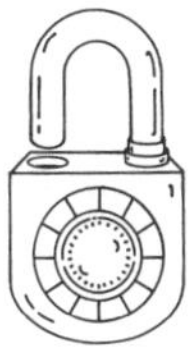

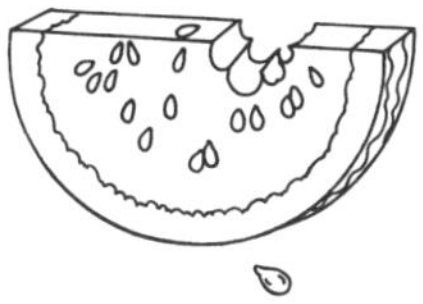

Name ______________________ Date ____________

Cut out the pictures and the book. Fold the book on the solid lines. Paste a *j* picture on each page and write its name. Read the sentence and do what it says.

Read It Together

Put an X on the hat.

My J j Book

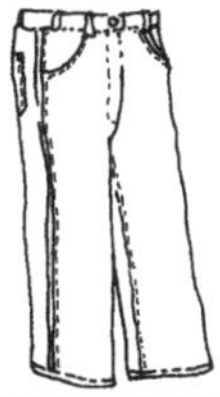

Name ______________________ Date ____________

Cut out the pictures and the book. Fold the book on the solid lines. Paste a *z* picture on each page and write its name. Read the sentence and do what it says.

Read It Together

Put an X on the wig.

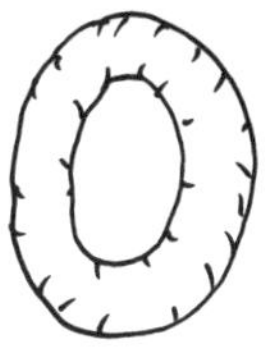

My Z z Book

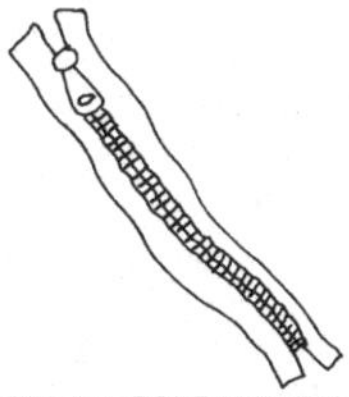

High Frequency Word Cards

get	day
help	from
of	good
put	she
we	us
work	very

Name ______________________ Date ____________

T-Chart

Compare Genres

Compare a story and a postcard.

Realistic Fiction	Postcard
is a made up story that seems real	is a message from a real person

Tell a partner how a story and a postcard are different.

Name ______________________ Date __________

Phonics

Letter and Sound Ee

Ee

Write the missing letter. Color each item named in the sentence.

1. 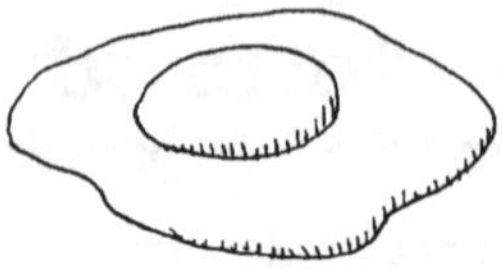 egg	**2.** 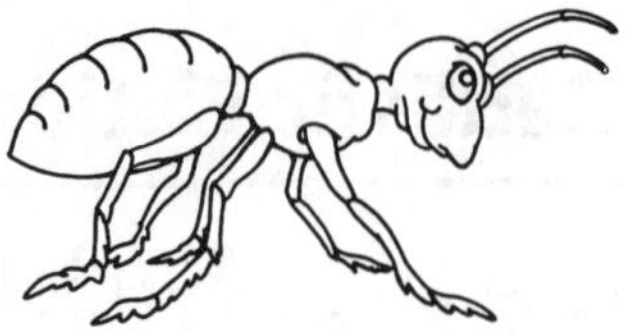 nt
3.  levator	**4.**  lbow
5.  nvelope	**6.**  orse

Read It Together Find the egg and the elbow.

Name ______________________ Date ____________

High Frequency Words

Zip Can Jog

Write a word from the box to complete each sentence.

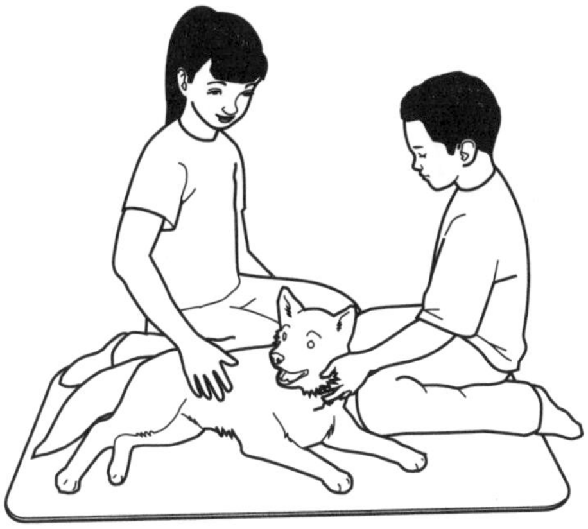

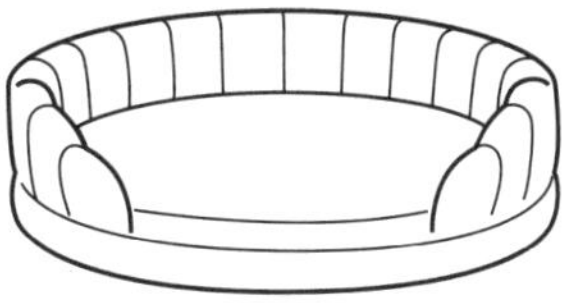

High Frequency **Words**
day
from
good
she
us
very

1. Zip is a ______________ dog.

2. Zip can jog ______________ the bed to the mat.

3. Zip can get a big pat from ______________.

4. ______________ can jog from the mat to the bed.

5. Zip has a very good ______________!

Name ______________________ Date ____________

Cut out the pictures and the book. Fold the book on the solid lines. Paste an *e* picture on each page and write its name. Read the sentence and do what it says.

Read It Together

Put an E on the leg.

My E e Book

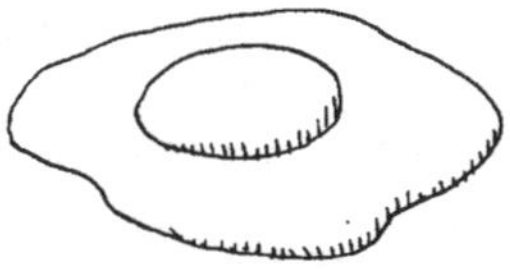

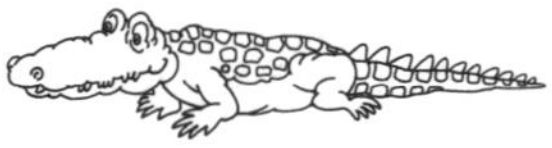

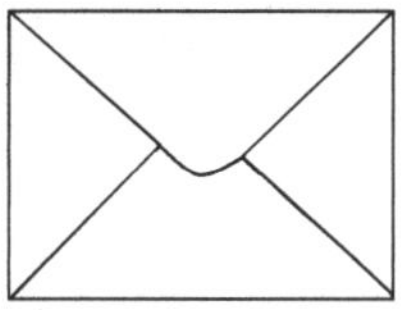

Name ______________________ Date ____________

Grammar and Writing

Proper Nouns and Dates

Look at each sentence. Circle the correct ending.

1. Jen lives in
   - seattle.
   - Seattle.

2. She lives with her mom and her brother
   - Tim.
   - tim.

3. Jen's family took a trip to
   - Texas.
   - texas.

4. They left on
   - July 18 2013.
   - July 18, 2013.

5. They came home the next
   - monday.
   - Monday.

6. Jen learned that Texas can be very hot in
   - july!
   - July!

Name ______________________________ Date ______________

Grammar: Proper Nouns

Name Game

Grammar Rules Proper Nouns

Start a proper noun with a capital letter. → My dog <u>Mac</u> is the best dog in the world.

1. **Play with a partner.**
2. **Spin the spinner.**
3. **Name a proper noun. Write the proper noun on a piece of paper.**

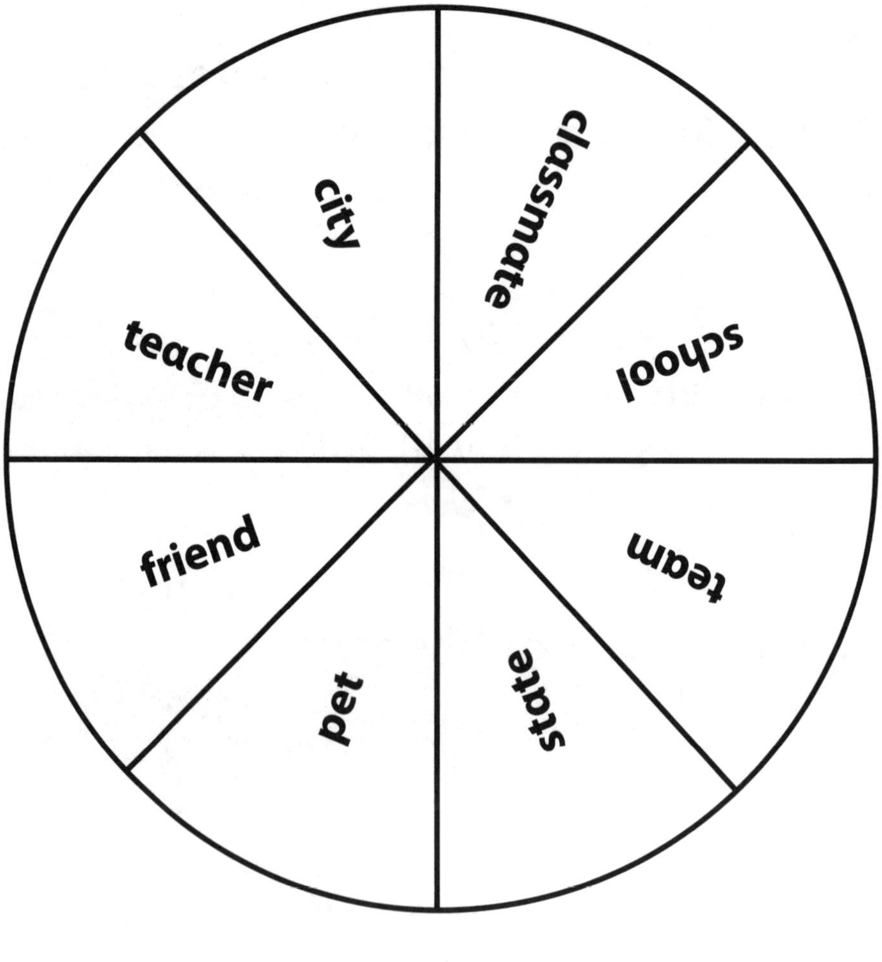

Make a Spinner

1. Put a paper clip in the center of the circle.
2. Hold one end of the paper clip with a pencil.
3. Spin the paper clip around the pencil.

Name ____________________ Date ____________

Prewrite Graphic Organizer: Idea Web

Idea Web

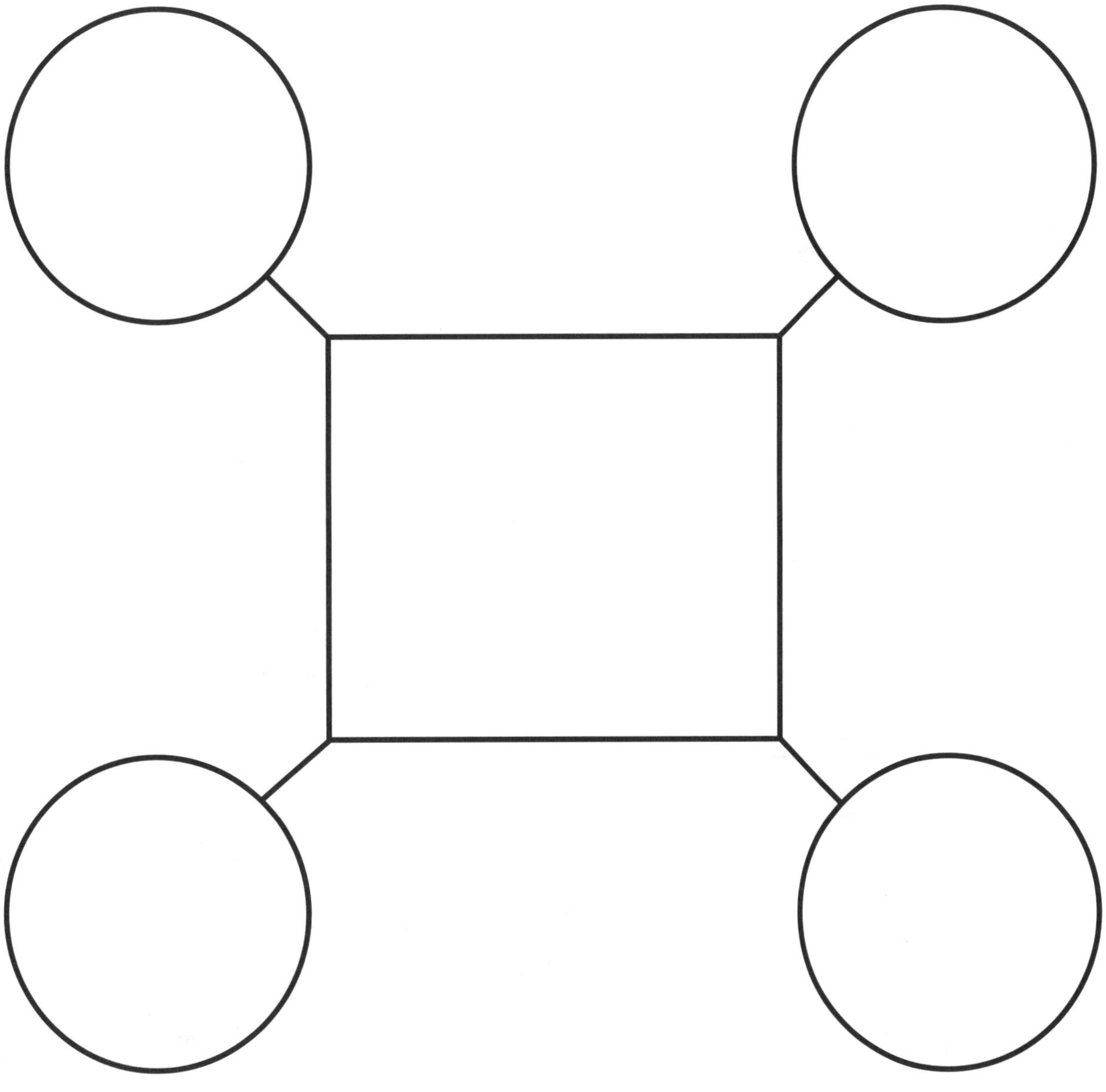

Word Choice Checklist

✓ Did you pick strong words?
✓ Do your words go with your pictures?
✓ Do your words grab your reader's attention?

Name ____________________ Date ____________

Phonics

Letter and Sound Yy

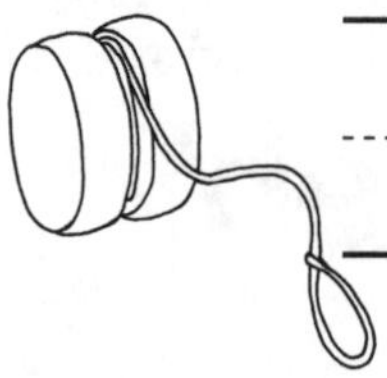

Yy

Name what is in each picture.
Write the missing letter.

1.

yarn

2.

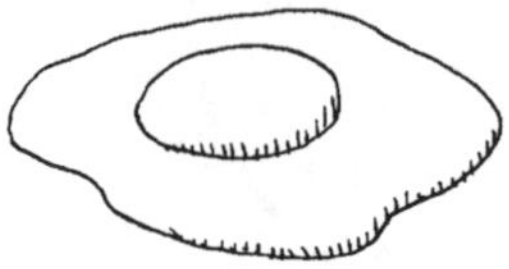

olk

3.

amp

4.

acht

5.

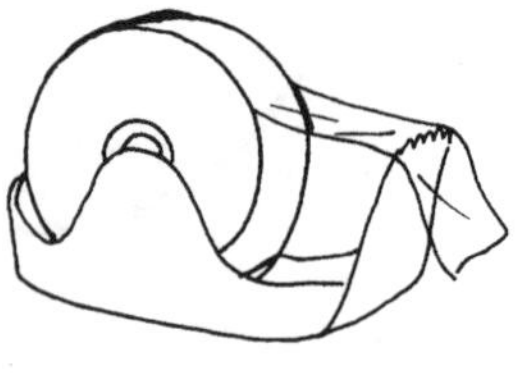

ape

6.

ut

Read It Together Can you find the nut? Yes, I can!

Name ____________________ Date ____________

Phonics

Letter and Sound Qq

Qq

Name what is in each picture. Write the missing letter.

1.

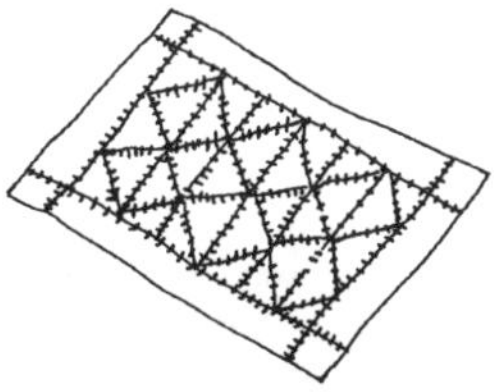

quilt

2.

_ave

3.

_ig

4.

_uarter

5.

_uart

6.

_ing

Read It Together Can I quit? Yes, you can.

Name ______________________ Date __________

Phonics

Letter and Sound Xx

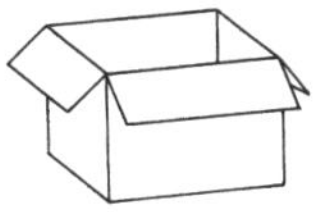

Xx

Cut out and name the picture cards. Trace the words. Put in the box the cards with names that end like *box*.

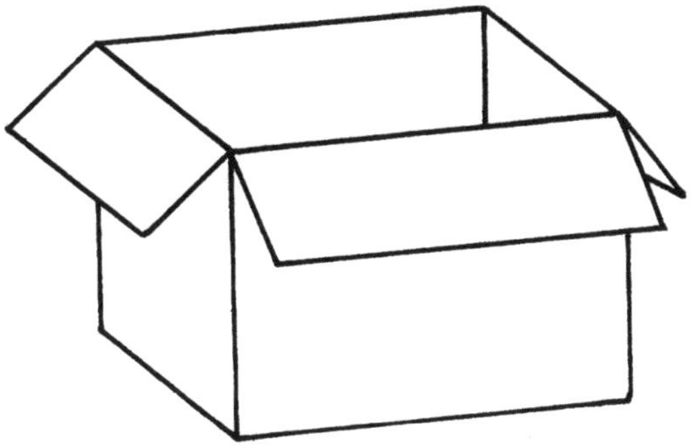

six

top

fox

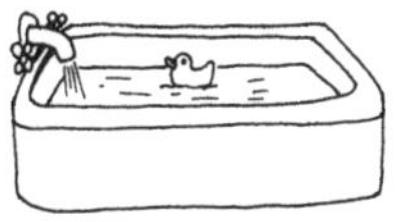

tub

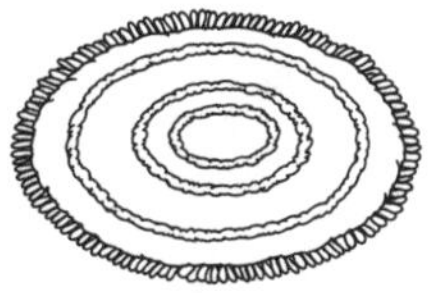

rug

ax

ox

pen

Read It Together What is in your box?

Name ______________________ Date ____________

Phonics

Letter and Sound Kk

Kk

Name what is in each picture. Write the missing letter.

1.  key	**2.**  obe	**3.**  it
4.  oll	**5.**  ing	**6.**  ox
7.  ite	**8.**  itten	**9.**  ake

Read It Together Find the kit and the fox.

Name ______________________ Date ______________

Checklist

List Facts

Use the checklist. Decide if something is living or nonliving.

Living Things Checklist	
can eat	☐
can drink	☐
is healthy	☐
can think	☐

Name ______________________ Date ____________

Phonics

Words with 's

Circle the word that completes each sentence. Write the word on the line. Read the sentences.

Sam **Sam's**

1. What is in ______________ box?

Jen **Jen's**

2. Mom finds ______________ cap in the box.

Dad **Dad's**

3. ______________ hat is in the box, too.

Quin **Quin's**

4. ______________ can not find his cat in the box.

Bev **Bev's**

5. The cat naps on ______________ mat.

Name ______________________________ Date ______________

Handwriting

High Frequency Words

Trace each word two times and then write it.

for for for

grow grow grow

keep keep keep

look look look

or or or

when when when

Name ______________________________ Date ____________

Cut out the pictures and the book. Fold the book on the solid lines. Paste a *y* picture on each page and write its name. Read the sentence and color what it names.

Read It Together

Find the yam.

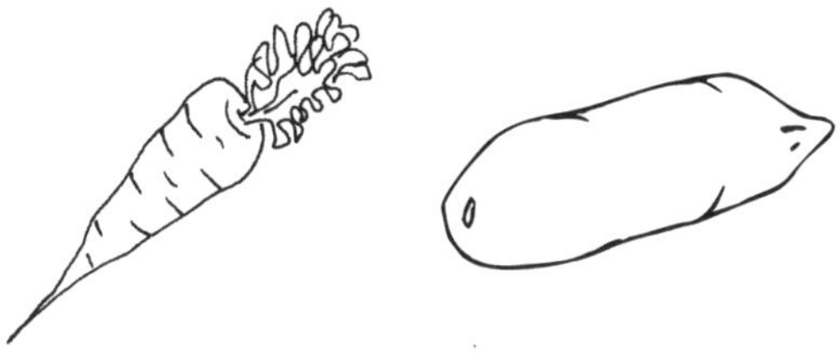

My Y y Book

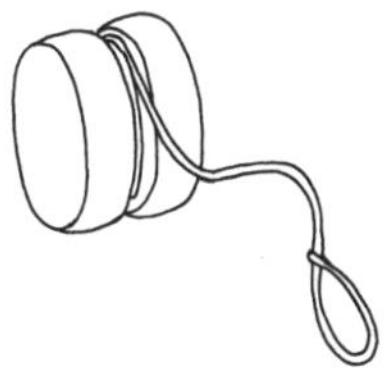

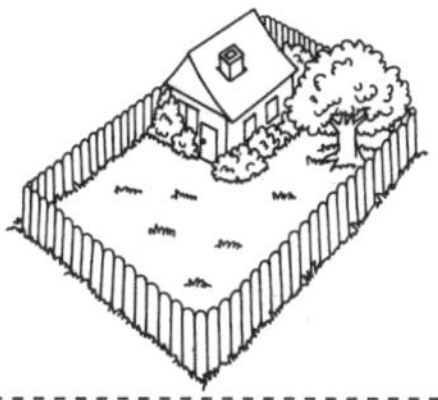

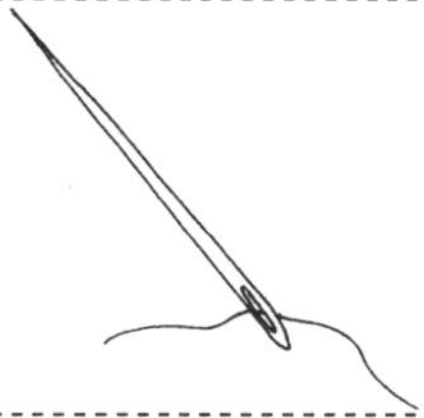

Name ______________________________ Date ______________

Cut out the pictures and the book. Fold the book on the solid lines. Paste a *q* picture on each page and write its name.

Read It Together

Is this a Q?
Yes, it is a big Q!

Q

My Q q Book

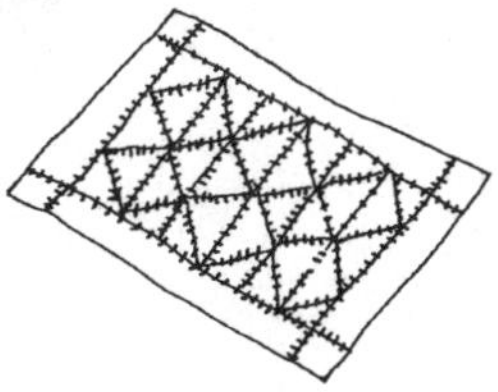

Name ______________________ Date ______________

Cut out the pictures and the book. Fold the book on the solid lines. Paste an *x* picture on each page and write its name. Draw a picture in the box that answers the question.

Read It Together

What do you have in a box?

My X x Book

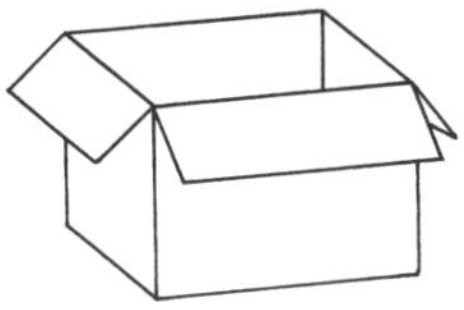

Name ______________________________ Date ______________

Cut out the pictures and the book. Fold the book on the solid lines. Paste a *k* picture on each page and write its name. Read the sentence and color what it names.

Read It Together

Find the kid.

My K k Book

Spelling & Word Work

High Frequency Word Cards

find	for
has	grow
have	keep
his	look
mother	or
too	when

Name ________________________ Date ____________

Phonics

Letter and Sound Uu

Uu

Name what is in each picture. Write the missing letter.

1.

umpire

2.

_pple

3.

_ouse

4.

_nderwear

5.

_ncle

6.

_eal

Read It Together Can a cub tug a tub in the mud?

Name ______________________ Date ____________

High Frequency Words

It Can Grow!

Look at the pictures. Write a word from the box to complete each sentence.

High Frequency **Words**
for
grow
keep
look
or
when

1. ____________ can Jen get a pup?

2. This little pup is a good pup ____________ Jen.

3. Jen can ____________ this little pup!

4. Look at the little pup ____________!

5. Is it a little pup ____________ a big dog?

Name ______________________ Date ______________

Grammar: Adjectives

Use Determiners

Cut out the words on the petals. Glue five petals around each center. Then make sentences with the word in the center and each petal.

that

those

these

this

hat	gloves	garden	hose
plant	shoes	shirt	pants
socks	kittens	dog	rabbit
glasses	pen	doors	window

Name ______________________ Date ____________

Cut out the pictures and the book. Fold the book on the solid lines. Paste a *u* picture on each page and write its name. Read the question and draw a picture.

Read It Together

Can a cub sit in the sun?

My U u Book

Name ______________________ Date ____________

Grammar & Writing

Write Adjectives

Read the story. Then choose a word from the box that goes with the sentence. Write it on the line.

this	that	these	those	fat	green

Amy looked at the garden. "What is that thing over by the fence?" she asked her mom. On the ground she saw a ____________ green worm. Her mom picked it up. She said, "____________ caterpillar is fat. It likes to eat ____________ plant stems. Her mom pointed to the last row of tomatoes. "I found many caterpillars on ____________ plants!" Then she looked down at the bean plants next to her feet. "I don't think the caterpillars like to eat ____________ beans," she said.

Name ______________________________ Date ____________

Vocabulary

Rivet

1. **Write the first letter of each word.**
2. **Have a partner try to guess the word.**
3. **Fill in letters one at a time until your partner guesses the word.**

1. ___ ___ ___ ___ ___ ___

2. ___ ___ ___

3. ___ ___ ___ ___ ___

4. ___ ___ ___ ___ ___ ___

5. ___ ___ ___ ___

6. ___ ___ ___ ___ ___ ___ ___

7. ___ ___ ___ ___ ___

8. ___ ___ ___ ___ ___ ___

9. ___ ___ ___ ___

10. ___ ___ ___ ___ ___ ___ ___ ___

11. ___ ___ ___ ___ ___ ___ ___ ___ ___

Take turns with a partner. Choose a word. Say it in a sentence.

Name ______________________ Date __________

Checklist

Are You Living?

Add facts you learned about living things to the checklist. Place checks in the boxes.

Living Things Checklist	
can eat	☐
can drink	☐
is healthy	☐
can think	☐
	☐
	☐
	☐
	☐

Take turns with a partner. Tell a fact that you learned about living things in "Are You Living?"

Name ______________________ Date ____________

Phonics

Double Consonants

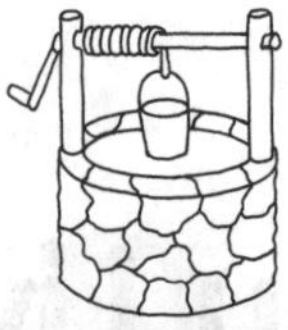

well

Name what is in each picture. Draw a line from the first letter to the rest of the word. Write the word and read it.

1.  og d oll doll	**2.**  uzz b oll	**3.** 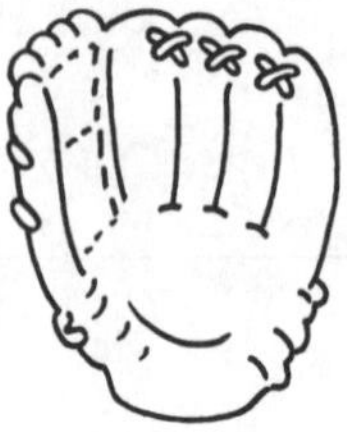 ill m itt
3.  oss t iff	**5.**  ell b ut	**6.**  uff h ill

Read It Together What can you toss to a pal with a mitt?

Name ______________________________ Date ______________

Phonics

Double Consonants

Cut along the dotted lines. Write *t, b, l, m* in each box of one pull strip and *b, f, s, y* in each box of the other. Put the strips through the slits with the arrows pointing up. Read the words you make.

toss

bell

oss

ell

Name ______________________________ Date ______________

Phonics

Blend Words

Name what is in each picture. Circle the word that goes with the picture.

1.  bed bell	**2.** 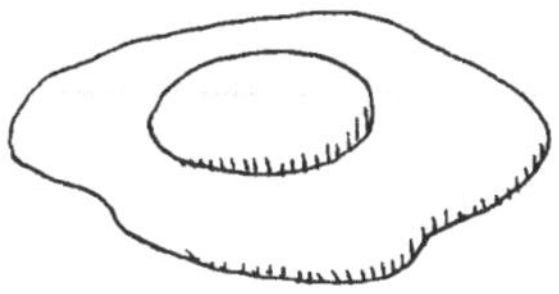 add egg	**3.**  us up
4.  an man	**5.** 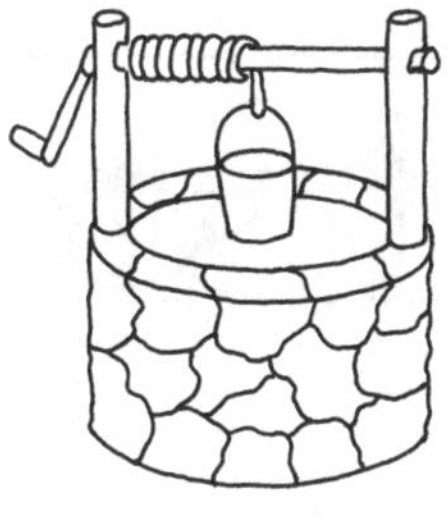 wax well	**6.** 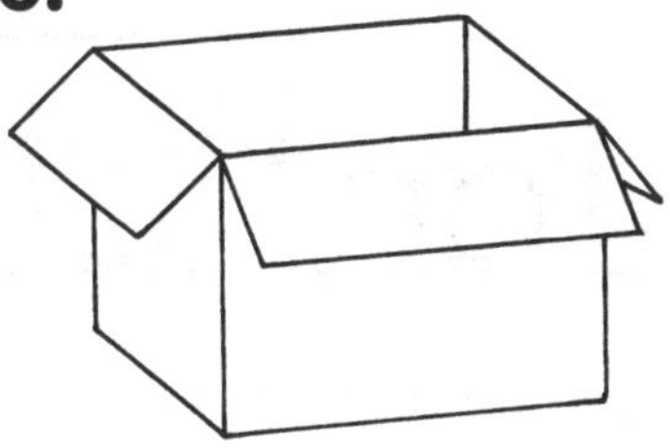 box ox
7.  hill hat	**8.**  is up	**9.**  ill if

Read It Together Can you put a bell in a box?

For use with TE p. T91c

Name ______________________ Date ____________

Handwriting

High Frequency Words

Trace each word two times and then write it.

body body body

how how how

out out out

start start start

they they they

use use use

Spelling & Word Work

Word Sort: Double Final Consonants

 egg	 bill	 doll	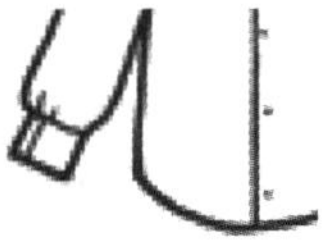 cuff
pass	puff	buzz	hiss
tell	odd	fuzz	fill
off	lass	mess	dull
fell	muss	will	huff
well	add	mill	jazz
yell	kiss	fizz	pill

Spelling & Word Work

High Frequency Word Cards

do	body
then	how
what	out
with	start
you	they
your	use

Name ______________________ Date ____________

T-Chart

Compare Genres

Compare a song and a diagram.

Song	Diagram
	has numbered steps

Work with a partner. Take turns asking about a song and a diagram.

Name ______________________ Date ____________

Phonics

Words with ck, ng

duck

sing

Name what is in each picture. Circle the word that goes with each picture.

1.

will
wing
wig

2.

taps
tan
tack

3.

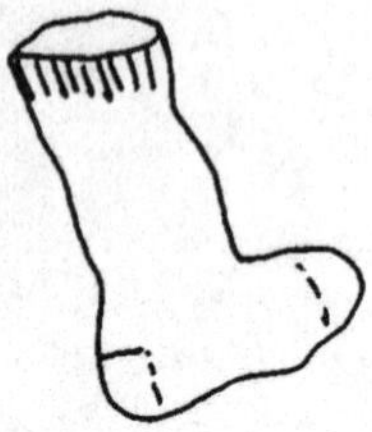

sock
sobs
song

4.

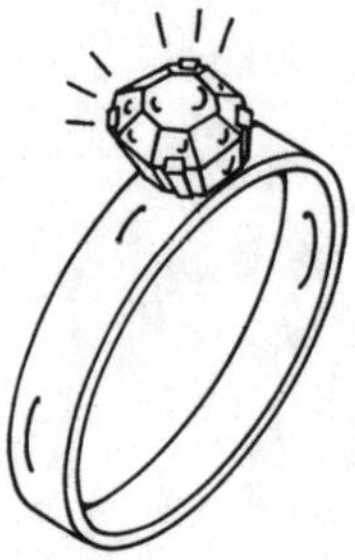

rip
ring
rock

5.

kill
kick
king

6.

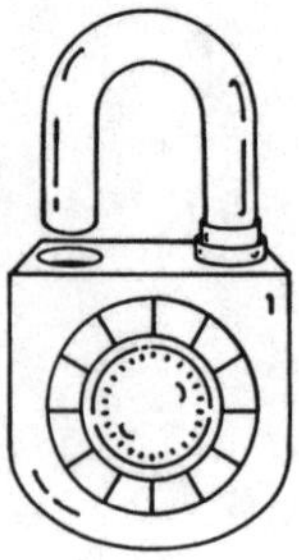

loss
lock
long

Read It Together A king has a ring. What has a wing?

Name ______________________ Date ____________

High Frequency Words

Tug, Tug, Tug

Look at the picture.
Write a word from the box to complete each sentence.

High Frequency Words
body
how
out
start
they
use

1. The dog can not get ______________!

2. His ______________ is too big.

3. ______________ will the dog get out?

4. Tom and Tim ______________ to help.

5. They ______________ rags and tug, tug, tug!

Name ______________________________ Date ______________

Grammar: Adjectives

Use Shades of Meaning

Read the adjective below each box. Then draw a picture in the box to show something that the adjective may describe. Here are some ideas you can draw.

apples	bugs	dogs	flowers	hats	shoes	trees	trucks

small	**tiny**	**itsy-bitsy**
big	**huge**	**enormous**

Name ______________________ Date ____________

Phonics

Words with ck, ng

Cut along the dotted lines. Write *d, l, r, s* in each box of one pull strip and *k, r, s, w* in each box of the other. Put the strips through the slits with the arrows pointing up. Read the words you make.

sock

wing

ock

ing

Name ______________________ Date ____________

Grammar & Writing

Write More Adjectives

Read the story. Then choose a word from the box that goes with the sentence. Write it on the line.

green	heavy	round	tiny

Jared and Paul planted a bag of seeds. "Wow," said Paul, "these seeds are so tiny, I can hardly see them." For a week, nothing happened. The boys kept watering the seeds. The watering can was ______________ and hard to lift. After a few weeks, they saw little ______________ leaves coming out of the soil. By the end of the month, they were eating delicious ______________ radishes.

Name ______________________ Date ____________

Grammar: Adjectives

Draw It!

Grammar Rules Adjectives

1. Adjectives describe how something looks.
2. Some adjectives tell about color, size, or shape.

The green plant is tall.

Read each sentence. Draw a line under each adjective. Then use the sentences to draw a picture on a separate piece on paper.

1. The park has green grass and yellow flowers.

2. Children play with a big, red ball.

3. A small, brown bird flies above.

4. A boy sees a blue house with square windows.

5. A tall man sells round balloons in many colors and sizes.

Take turns with a partner. Show your picture and describe it.

Name ______________________ Date __________

Phonics

Blends fl, pl, sl

flag

plug

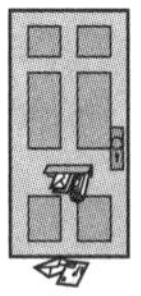
slot

Name what is in each picture. Circle the word that goes with each picture.

1.

flag

bag

wag

2.

us

fuss

plus

3.

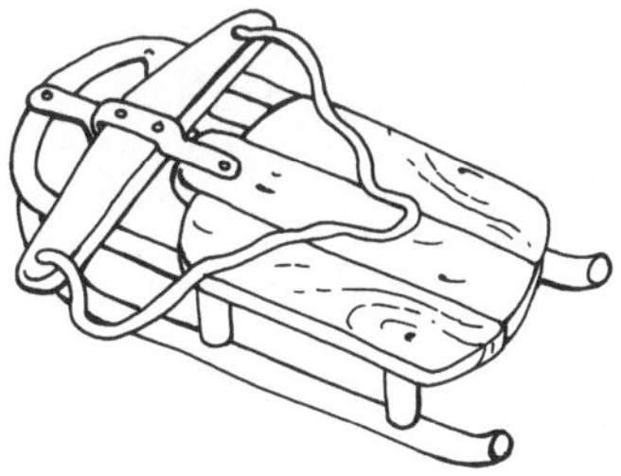

led

sled

fled

4.

hum

slum

plum

5.

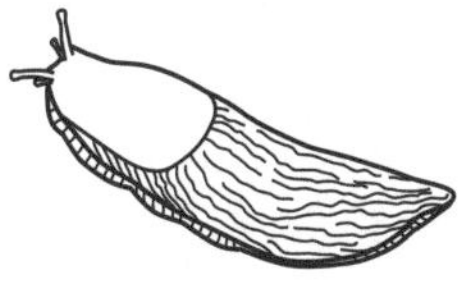

plug

lug

slug

6.

flock

lock

sock

Read It Together Find a flag and a slug.

Name ______________________________ Date ____________

Character-Setting-Plot Chart

Identify Plot

Retell a story you know to a partner. Fill out the chart.

Title: ______________________________

Character:

Character:

Setting:

Plot:

Name ______________________ Date ____________

Phonics

Blends fl, pl, sl

Name what is in each picture. Draw a line from the blends on the left to the rest of the word. Write the word and read it.

1.

sl — ed / ot

slot

2.

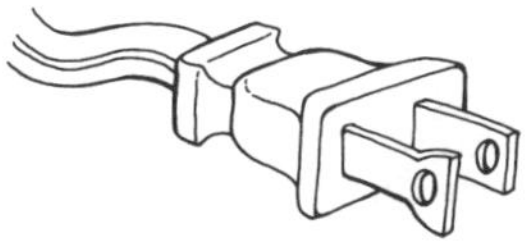

pl — um / ug

3.

fl — at / ag

4.

pl — us / uck

5.

fl — ock / ick

6.

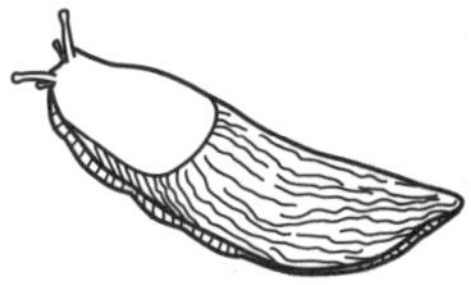

sl — id / ug

Read It Together Sid and Sam slid on the sled.

Name ______________________ Date ____________

Phonics

Blend words

Circle the word that names each picture. Read the word.

1.

slam slip

2.

plum plan

3.

flap flag

4.

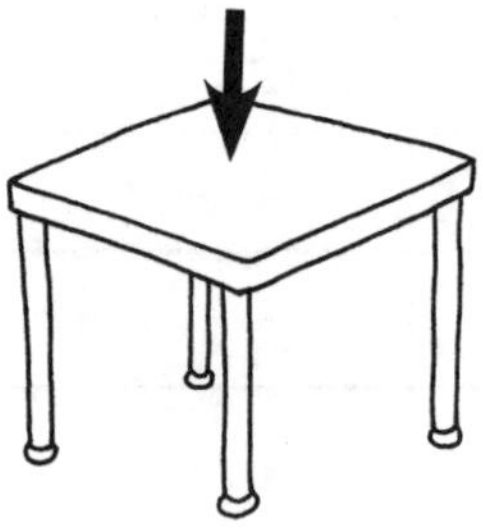

flat slat

5.

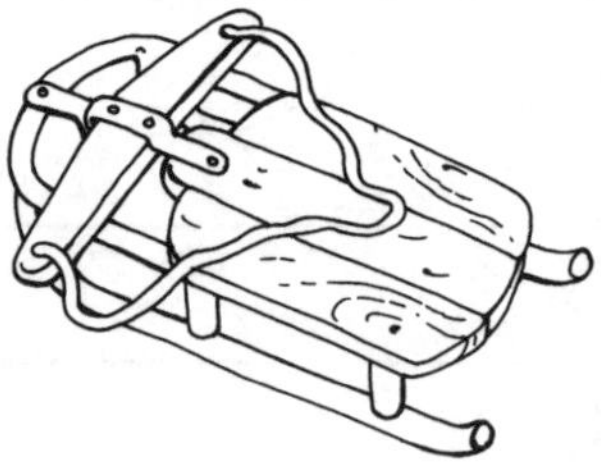

fled sled

6.

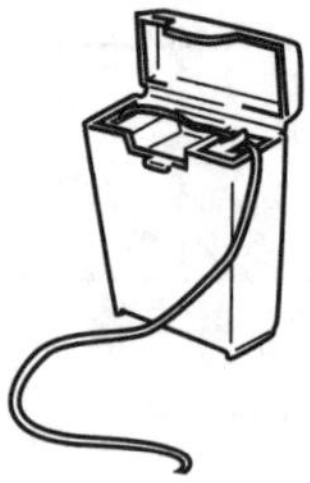

floss flex

7.

slot slid

8.

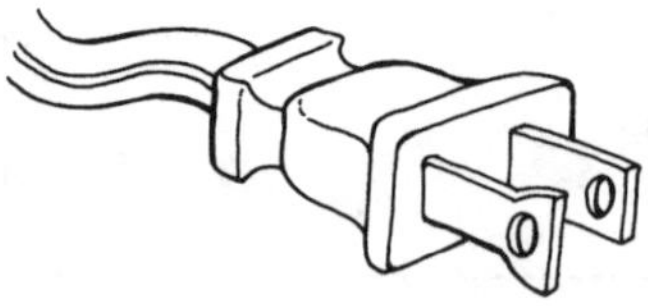

plan plug

9.

plum fluff

Read It Together It is flat. Can it flap?

Name ____________________ Date ____________

Handwriting

High Frequency Words

Trace each word two times and then write it.

does does does

eat eat eat

live live live

no no no

see see see

why why why

Spelling & Word Work

Word Cards: *fl, pl, sl*

 flag	 plug	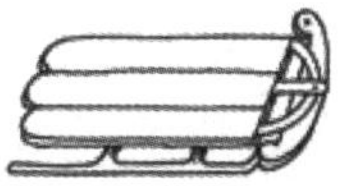 sled	 flock
fling	flip	flat	slit
flap	plan	plum	slip
plus	flick	slick	slam
slap	slop	flop	fled
pluck	slim	fluff	slung
sling	plop	slug	fleck

High Frequency Word Cards

get	does
help	eat
of	live
put	no
we	see
work	why

Name ______________________ Date ____________

Phonics

Blends cl, gl, bl

class

glob

block

Circle the word that names each picture. Read the word.

1.

cap
flap
clap

2.

black
flack
back

3.

glad
lad
clad

4.

lock
clock
flock

5.

gas
class
glass

6.

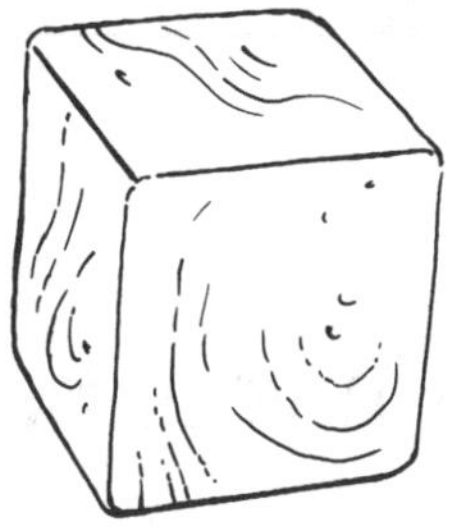

click
block
flick

Read It Together Do you clap when you are glad?

Name ______________________ Date ______________

High Frequency Words

What Is It?

Look at the picture. Write a word from the box to complete each sentence.

High Frequency Words
does
eat
live
no
see
why

1. ______________ it start in an egg? Yes!

2. Do you ______________ it peck? Yes!

3. Yum! Will it ______________ a bug? Yes!

4. Can it live in your bed? ______________, it can not!

5. ______________ not? It is a hen!

Grammar: Adjectives

Word Cards: Adjectives

some	a lot	much	a little
many	a few	three	six
hat	glove	garden	water
shovel	bread	dirt	air
plant	shoe	shirt	seed
wind	kitten	dog	rain
glasses	pen	food	furniture
snow	plate	apple	banana

Name ______________________ Date ____________

Phonics

Blends cl, gl, bl

Draw a line from the blend on the left to the rest of the word. Write the word and read it.

1.	2.	3.
		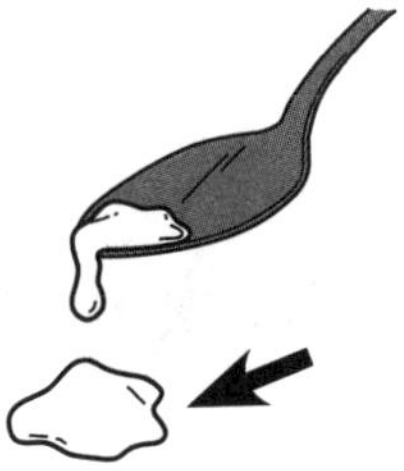
cl ip / iff — clip	gl ad / um	gl ob / ad

4.	5.	6.
	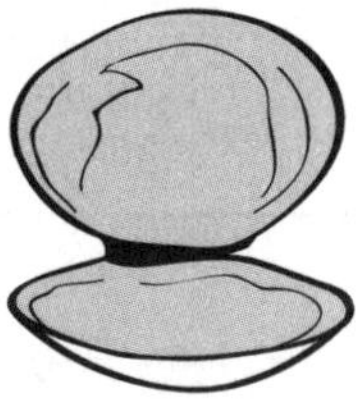	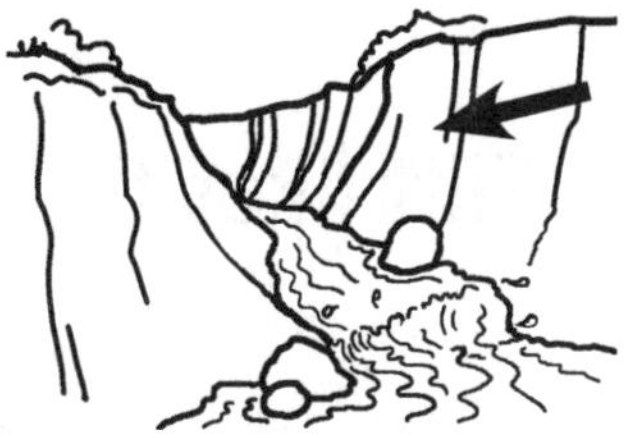
bl ot / ess	cl am / ub	bl ab / uff

Read It Together Do you use black blocks and clips in class?

Name ______________________ Date ____________

Phonics

Short a, i

Circle the word that completes each sentence.
Write the word on the line. Read the sentences.

quick **quack**

1. A duck likes to ______________ .

flap **slip**

2. A duck likes to ______________ its wings, too.

3. What does Cliff like to do?

sing **sang**

Cliff likes to ______________ .

clip **clap**

4. Pam likes to ______________ for Cliff.

5. What does a dog like to do?

yam **yip**

It likes to ______________ and yap!

Name ______________________ Date ____________

Grammar & Writing

Write Indefinite Adjectives

Read the letter. Then choose a word from the box that goes with each sentence.

a few	a little	many	much	some

Hi Uncle Ray,

Did you hear that we are planting a garden this year? Last year, some friends gave us only a few tomatoes, but that was not enough for us. It was so ______________ work to plant everything. If we get ______________ rain, I'm sure our plants will grow. I hope we get ______________ tomatoes this year. I love to eat them with ______________ salt.

Love,
Amber

Name ______________________________ Date ______________

Vocabulary

Around the World

1. **The traveler stands behind a challenger.**
2. **Listen to the clue. Find the Key Word and say it.**
3. **The first to answer correctly travels to the next student on the right. The first traveler to go all around the circle wins.**

KEY WORDS

seed	bud	petal	flower	leaf

CLUES

- a part of a plant that is the start of a flower
- the flat, green part of a plant
- the flat part of a flower
- a part of a plant that is small and grows into a new plant
- a part of a plant that has many petals

Name ______________________ Date ____________

Character-Setting-Plot Chart

The Daisy

Complete the chart. Describe what happens to the little seed in "The Daisy."

Character: raindrop

Character: sun

Character: little seed

Setting: outside in the country

Plot:

Take turns with a partner. Use your chart to describe what happens to the little seed.

Name ______________________ Date ____________

Phonics

Blends fr, gr, tr

frog

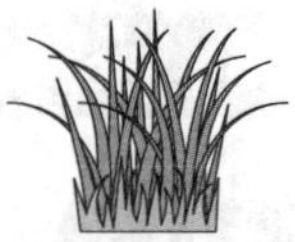
grass

truck

Circle the word that goes with each picture. Read the word.

1.

fog
frog
flag

2.

track
tuck
pluck

3.

trot
frizz
class

4.

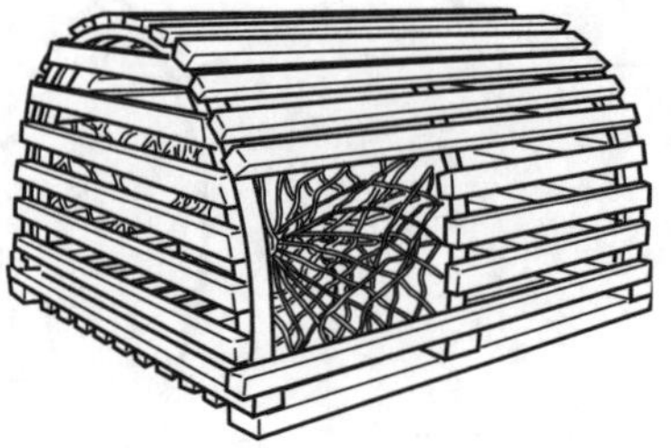

tap
trap
flap

5.

gas
glass
grass

6.

grub
rub
club

Read It Together We can see a grub in the grass.

Name ______________________ Date ____________

Phonics

Blends fr, gr, tr

Draw a line from the blend on the left to the rest of the word. Write the word and read it.

1.

gr — ip / in

grin

2.

tr — ick / uck

3.

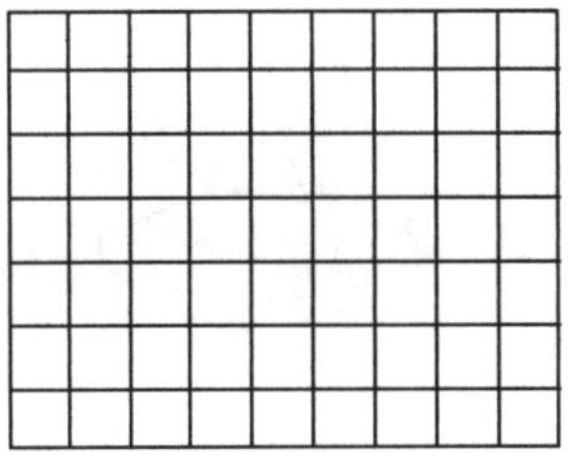

gr — ill / id

4.

fr — og / izz

5.

tr — ap / ip

6.

Gr — ip / an

Read It Together Tran trots to the truck.

Name ______________________________ Date ______________

Phonics

Blend words

Circle the word that goes with each picture. Read the word.

1.

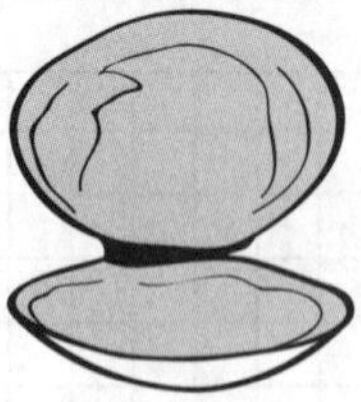

club clam

2.

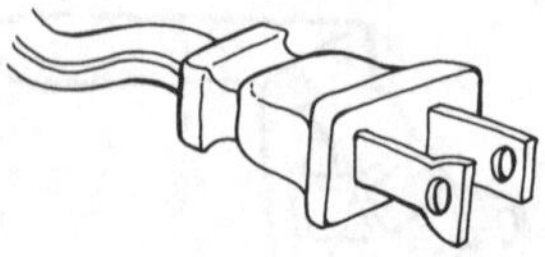

slug plug

3.

clock click

4.

plus plan

5.

clog frog

6.

plot glob

7.

block black

8.

grin grip

9.

flag flat

Read It Together The black clock ticks and tocks.

Name ______________________ Date ____________

Handwriting

High Frequency Words

Trace each word two times and then write it.

all all all

are are are

by by by

first first first

more more more

there there there

Spelling & Word Work

Word Cards: *fr, gr, tr, br, cr, dr*

 frog	 grass	 truck	 drop
frill	dress	drank	crop
grab	grow	grin	grunt
drill	crab	trim	trap
frizz	grub	gruff	drip
trip	grid	brim	brink
grip	crib	cram	Fred

Spelling & Word Work

High Frequency Word Cards

day	all
from	are
good	by
she	first
us	more
very	there

Name ______________________ Date ____________

T-Chart

Compare Genres

Compare a fairy tale and a project notebook.

Fairy Tale	Project Notebook
is a fantasy	is nonfiction

Take turns with a partner. Tell how a fairy tale is different than a project notebook.

Name ______________________ Date ____________

Phonics

Blends br, cr, dr

brick

crab

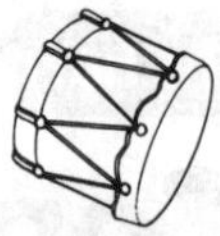
drum

Circle the word that goes with each picture. Read the word.

1.

slim
grim
brim

2.

rib
crib
drill

3.

dress
press
brass

4.

grip
drop
crop

5.

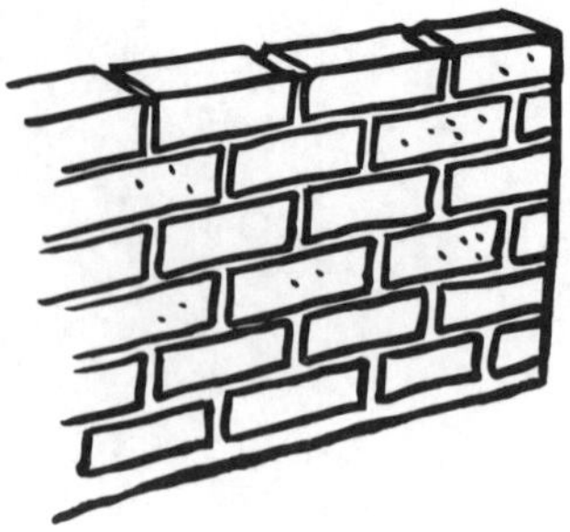

tricks
bricks
clicks

6.

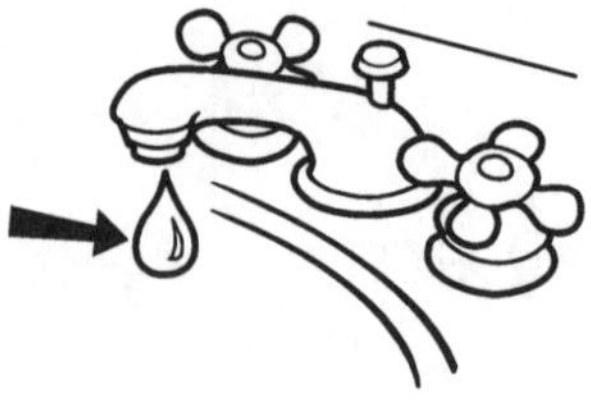

drip
grip
trip

Read It Together Grab that brick, and do not drop it.

Name ______________________________ Date ______________

High Frequency Words

Yum!

Look at the pictures. Write a word from the box to complete each sentence.

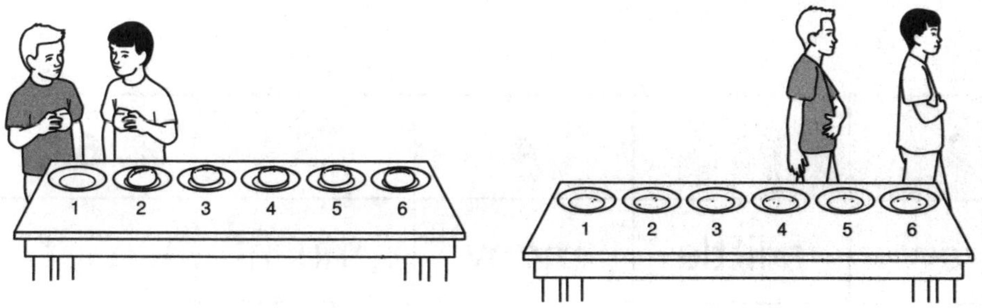

High Frequency Words
all
are
by
first
more
there

1. There ______________ six buns.

2. Matt and Bill pass ______________ the buns.

3. They eat the ______________ bun.

4. Then they eat ______________ the buns!

5. There are no ______________ buns.

Name ______________________ Date ____________

Grammar: Adjectives

Use Indefinite Adjectives

Use a number cube with six numbers to play the game. Roll the cube and find your number on the chart.

Chart

1	2	3	4	5	6
some	a few	a little	many	much	a lot

Say a sentence using the word that matches your number. If all of the players agree that your sentence is correct, mark it off on the score sheet.

Score Sheet

Player 1 __________ Player 2 __________ Player 3 __________

1		1		1	
2		2		2	
3		3		3	
4		4		4	
5		5		5	
6		6		6	

Name ______________________ Date __________

Phonics

Blends br, cr, dr

Draw a line from the blend on the left to the rest of the word. Write the word and read it.

1.

cr — ops / oss

cross

2.

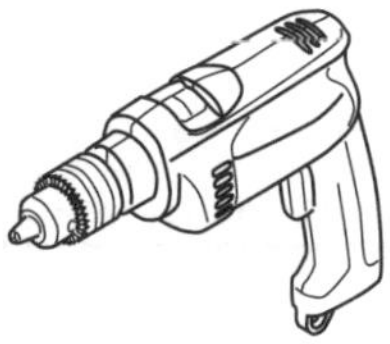

dr — ag / ill

3.

cr — ib / ack

4.

dr — op / ess

5.

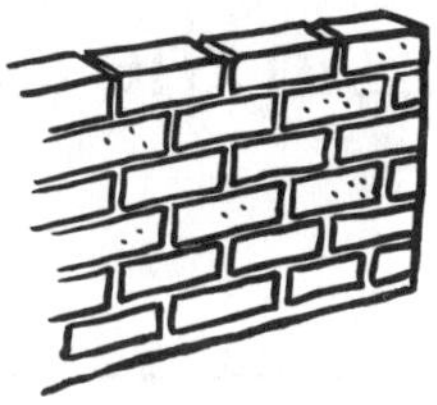

br — icks / ag

6.

br — ing / im

Read It Together Fred brings a brass drum.

Name ______________________ Date ____________

Phonics

Short o, e, u

Circle the word that completes each sentence.
Write the word on the line. Read the sentences.

red **rod**

1. Fred has a little ______________ hen.

clocks **clucks**

2. Fred's hen ______________ a lot.

pecks **pucks**

3. It ______________ in the mud, too.

begs **bugs**

4. The hen finds ______________ to eat. Yum!

5. The hen does not like to eat

crops **cribs**

Fred's ______________ !

Name ____________________ Date __________

Grammar & Writing

Write Indefinite Adjectives

Read the play. Then choose a word from the box that goes with each sentence.

some	a little	many	how many	how much

Kala is helping her father work in the family garden.

Father: Kala, please pour a little water on that row of beans. Not too much.

Kala: ____________ plants look yellow and dry.

____________ rain do we need?

Father: I think three or four days of rain will really help our plants.

Kala: ____________ hours have we been working in the sun?

Father: Maybe it's time to stop. Let's go get ____________ ice cream.

Name ______________________ Date ____________

Grammar: Adjectives

At School

Grammar Rules Adjectives

1. Some adjectives tell how many there are of something.

   I ate three pears.

2. Some adjectives tell how much there is of something.

   I need some water.

Complete the sentences below. Use words from the box.

much	some	five	many	ten

1. There are many books in the library.
2. There are ______ soccer balls in the gym.
3. There is ______ food in the cafeteria.
4. There is not ______ milk in the cafeteria.
5. There are ______ pencils on the desk.

Write two sentences about your school. Use adjectives. Read them to a partner.

Name ____________________ Date __________

Prewrite Graphic Organizer: Steps in a Process Diagram

Steps in a Process Diagram

Materials: ______________________________

____

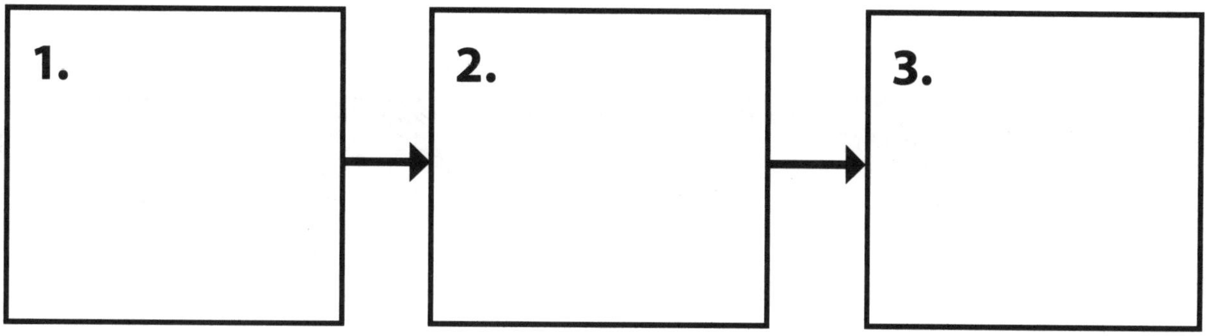

Organization Checklist

✓ Did you list what you need?
✓ Did you write what to do?
✓ Did you list the steps in order?
✓ Did you number the steps?

Name ______________________ Date ____________

Phonics

Blends with s

spot

swing

sling

Circle the word that names each picture. Read and answer the question. Act out each action.

1.

slim

skim

swim

2.

spin

grin

skin

3.

sped

sled

slug

4.

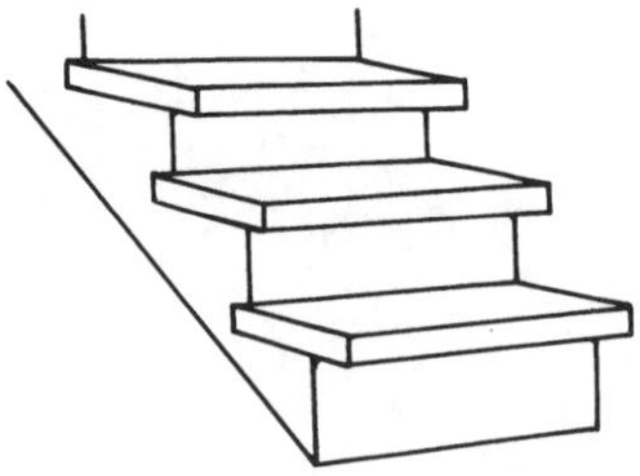

steps

snaps

scabs

5.

snip

slip

skip

6.

spell

smell

swell

Read It Together Can you skip, swim, spin, and sled?

Name ______________________________ Date ______________

T-Chart

Categorize Needs and Wants

List what you need and what you want in the T-chart below.

Need	Want
• peas	• toy car
• fish	• ball
•	•
•	•
•	•

Name ______________________ Date __________

Phonics

Blends with s

Draw a line from the first two letters to the rest of the word. Write the word and read it. Read the sentence.

1.

sp — ell / ot

spot

2.

sw — im / ing

3.

st — em / op

4.

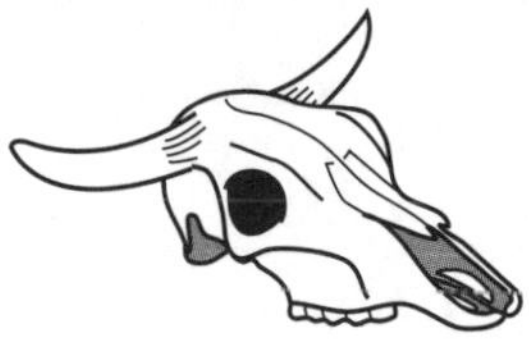

sk — ull / ip

5.

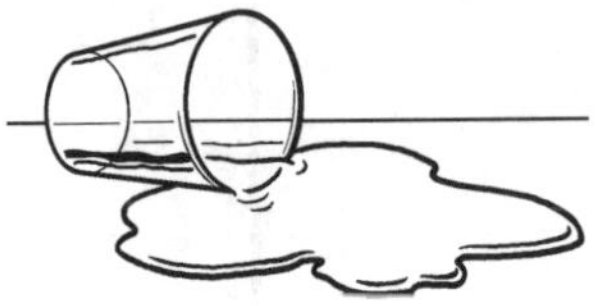

sp — in / ill

6.

sl — ing / ug

Read It Together Stan sees a slug on the swing.

Name ______________________ Date ______________

Handwriting

High Frequency Words

Trace each word two times and then write it.

go go go

great great great

one one one

saw saw saw

want want want

would would would

Spelling & Word Work

Word Cards: Words with *s* Blends

 stack	 snack	 swim	 sled
smack	spot	skill	swamp
step	smell	sling	skip
spill	swell	skid	stem
spend	skin	slam	smart
swing	slid	spin	sniff
snap	snug	stuck	small

Spelling & Word Work

High Frequency Word Cards

for	go
grow	great
keep	one
look	saw
or	want
when	would

Name ______________________________ Date ____________

Phonics

Triple Blends with s

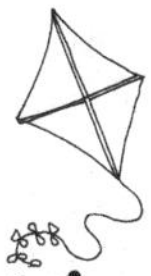

string

Circle the word that names the picture. Read the sentence.

1.

snub
scrub
sub

2.

snip
scram
strum

3.

spring
sling
string

4.

strong
scram
swing

5.

slug
sprig
sprung

6.

scrap
stuck
struck

Read It Together The strong cat springs to get the string.

Name ______________________ Date __________

High Frequency Words

The Sled

Look at the picture. Write a word from the box to complete each sentence.

High Frequency Words
go
great
one
saw
want
would

1. What did I see? I ______________ sleds on a hill.

2. My pal slid on ______________ sled.

3. I ______________ to get a sled, too.

4. I ______________ get on it and go, go, go!

5. I would have ______________ fun on my sled!

Name ______________________ Date ____________

Grammar

Use Action Verbs

1. Toss two markers on the game board. Toss one marker on the left side and one marker on the right side.
2. Say the word or words on the left. Name the action in the picture on the right.
3. Use the words in a sentence.
4. Play until each player has said five sentences.

He	
She	
The boy	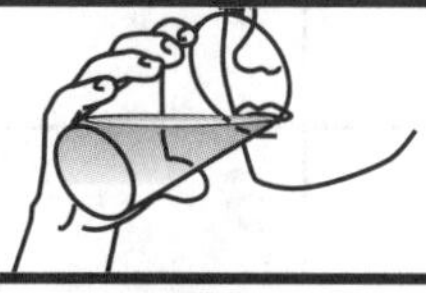
The Girl	
The man	
The woman	
The apple	
It	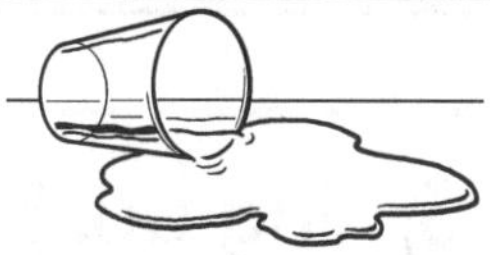

Name ______________________ Date ____________

Phonics

Triple Blends with s

Name the picture. Draw a line from the first three letters to the rest of the word. Write the word and read it. Read and act out the sentences.

1.

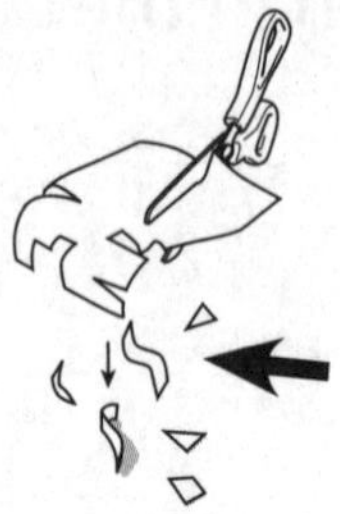

scr ····· aps

ams

scraps

2.

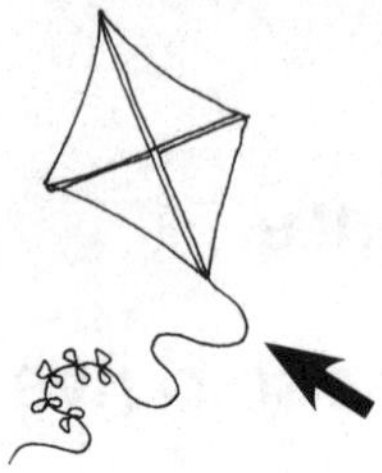

str

ess

ing

3.

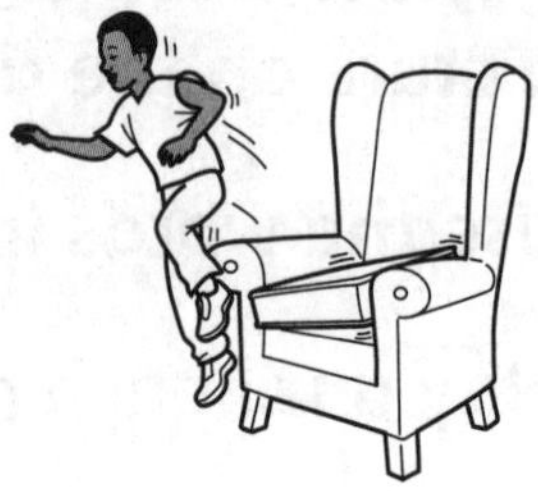

spr

ing

ig

4.

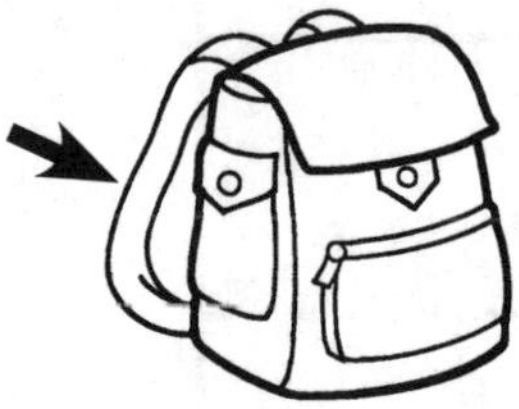

str

ap

ut

5.

scr

uff

ub

6.

spr

ung

ig

Read It Together Spring up. Scrub up. Strut off.

Name ______________________ Date ____________

Phonics

Endings -s, -ing

Take one card. Find the person with a card that has the same word on it, even if that word has a different ending. Say the words and use them in a sentence.

kick	**kicks**
quack	**quacks**
smell	**smells**
swing	**swinging**
sniff	**sniffing**
duck	**ducking**

Name ______________________ Date ____________

Grammar and Writing

Write Present Tense Verbs

Subject	Action Verb
I	eat
We	shop
You	buy
They	sell
The girls	walk
He	eats
She	sells
It	walks
The boy	buys
The tree	grows

Read each sentence. Circle the correct verb. Write the verb.

1. We ________ through the market. walk / walks
2. The man ________ fruit. sell / sells
3. Kate ________ an orange. buy / buys
4. Tom and I ________ grapes. buy / buys
5. Kate ________ her orange. eat / eats
6. We ________ our grapes. eat / eats
7. They ________ fast. disappear / disappears

Name ______________________ Date __________

Vocabulary

Rivet

1. **Write the first letter of each word.**
2. **Try to guess the word.**
3. **Fill in the other letters of the word.**

1. ___ ___ ___ ___ ___

2. ___ ___ ___ ___ ___

3. ___ ___ ___ ___ ___ ___

4. ___ ___ ___ ___ ___

5. ___ ___ ___

6. ___ ___ ___ ___ ___ ___ ___ ___

7. ___ ___ ___ ___ ___

8. ___ ___ ___

9. ___ ___ ___ ___

10. ___ ___ ___ ___

Take turns with a partner. Choose a word. Say it in a sentence.

Name ______________________ Date ______________

T-chart

Markets

List types of markets that you read about. List what each market sells in the What It Sells column.

Type of Market	What It Sells
• fruit market	• bananas, pears, grapes
•	•
•	•
•	•

Take turns with a partner. Tell what you learned about markets. Use your T-chart.

Name ______________________________ Date ______________

Phonics

Final nd, nk, nt

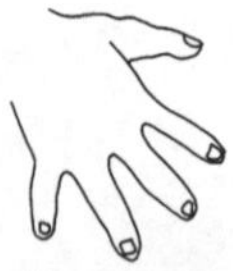
hand

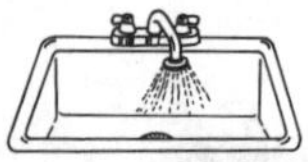
sink

tent

Circle the word that names the picture. Read and answer the question.

1.

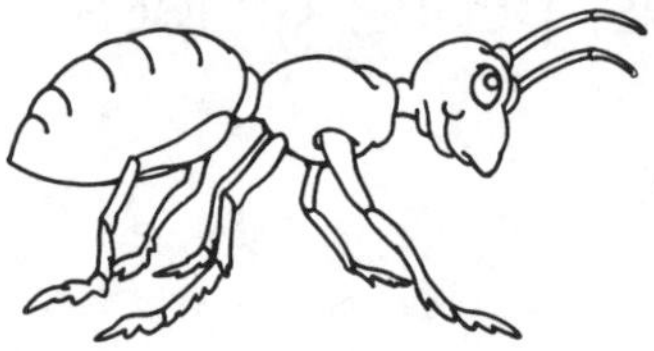

and

ant

ax

2.

skunk

skin

skull

3.

plant

plank

plan

4.

pick

pink

pond

5.

bend

bell

bed

6.

back

bank

band

Read It Together Does Hank see a skunk or an ant by the pond?

Name ______________________ Date ____________

Phonics

Final nd, nk, nt

Write the letters to complete the word. Read and answer the question.

1.

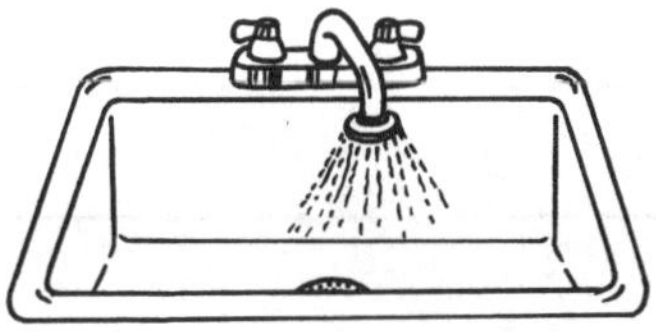

sink

2.

te

3.

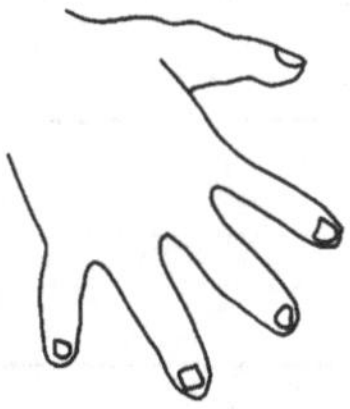

ha

4.

tru

5.

pla

6.

po

Read It Together Can you put a hand or a trunk in the sink?

Name ______________________ Date ____________

Handwriting

High Frequency Words

Trace each word two times and then write it.

give give give

he he he

know know know

said said said

watch watch watch

who who who

Spelling & Word Work

Word Cards: Final Blends *-nd, -nk, -nt, -st, -mp, -ft, -sk, -lt*

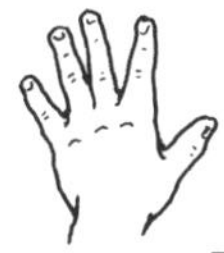 hand	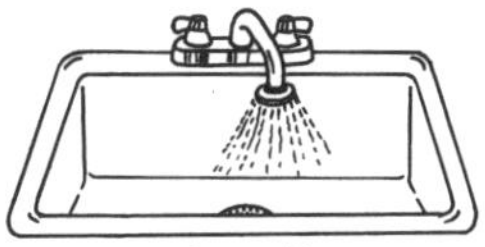 sink	 tent	 lamp
lift	honk	tank	best
mint	ask	cost	send
went	felt	gift	wilt
raft	pond	skunk	stamp
hint	melt	fast	stand
romp	whisk	mask	theft

Spelling & Word Work

High Frequency Word Cards

body	give
how	he
out	know
start	said
they	watch
use	who

Name ______________________ Date ____________

Three-Column Chart

Compare Authors' Purpose

Compare the authors' purposes in the social studies and online articles.

	Markets	Flower Power
Topic	markets around the world	
Author's Purpose		

Tell a partner how the authors' purposes in the social studies and online articles are alike and different.

Name ______________________________ Date ______________

Phonics

More Final Blends

nest lamp gift desk belt

Circle the word that names the picture. Read and answer the question.

1.

lick

lift

list

2.

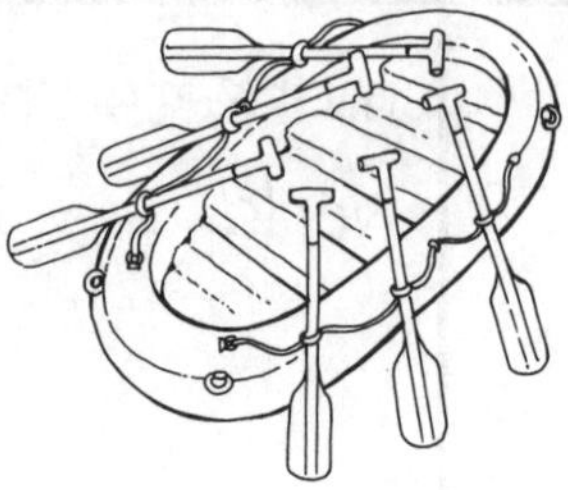

ramp

raft

rat

3.

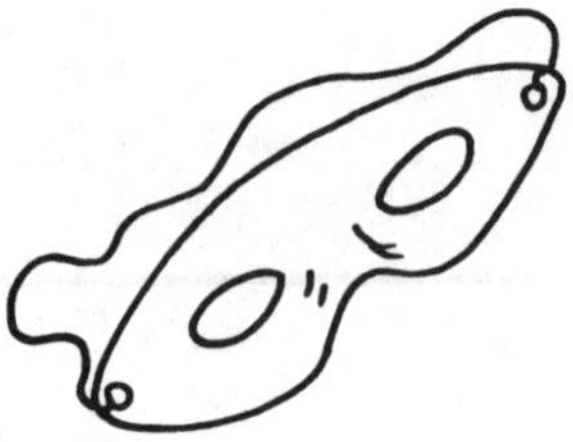

mat

mast

mask

4.

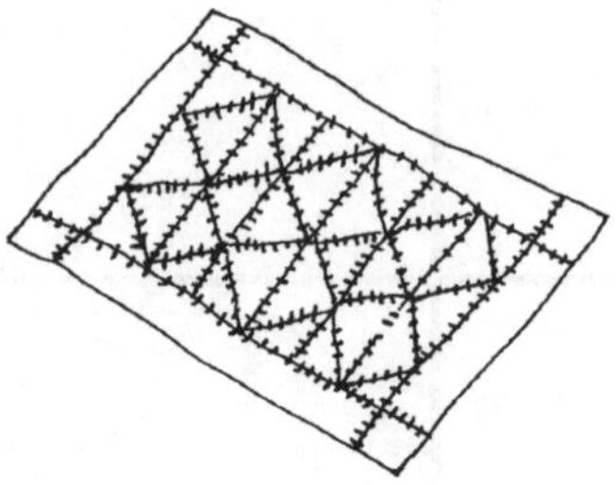

quilt

quick

quack

5.

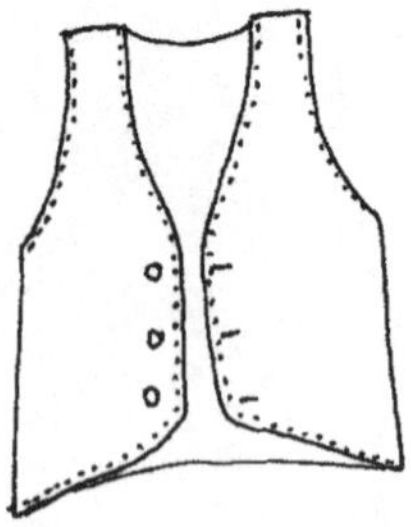

vend

vent

vest

6.

cap

camp

cast

Read It Together Do you want a mask, a vest, or a belt for a gift?

Name ______________________ Date ____________

High Frequency Words

The Raft

Look at the picture. Write a word from the box to complete each sentence. Read the sentences.

High Frequency **Words**
give
he
know
said
watch
who

1. Dad ____________ that he wants a raft.

2. We ____________ him one for a gift!

3. Do you ____________ if we can go on the raft with Dad?

4. Dad asks ____________ wants to go with him.

5. Tess and I go. Mom and Frank sit on the bank and ____________.

Name ______________________ Date ____________

Grammar: Present Tense

Talk About Routines

Grammar Rules Routines

A routine word like always, usually, sometimes, or never tells how often someone does something.

The boy sometimes sings in the morning.

1. **Play with a partner.**
2. **Spin the spinner.**
3. **Tell about the person in the picture. Use a routine word and the present tense.**

Make a Spinner

1. Put a paper clip in the center of the circle.
2. Hold one end of the paper clip with a pencil.
3. Spin the paper clip around the pencil.

Name ______________________ Date ____________

Phonics

More Final Blends

Write the letters to complete the words. Read and act out the sentences.

1.

melt

2.

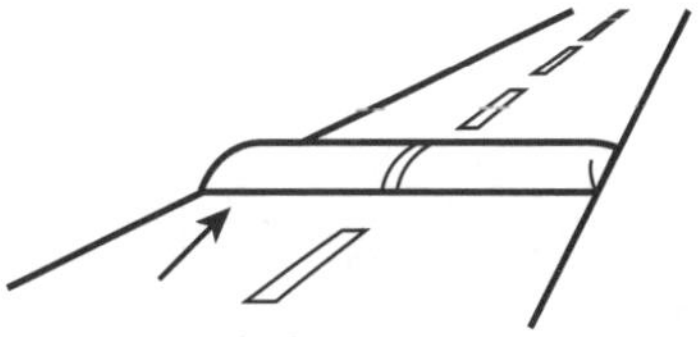

bu

3.

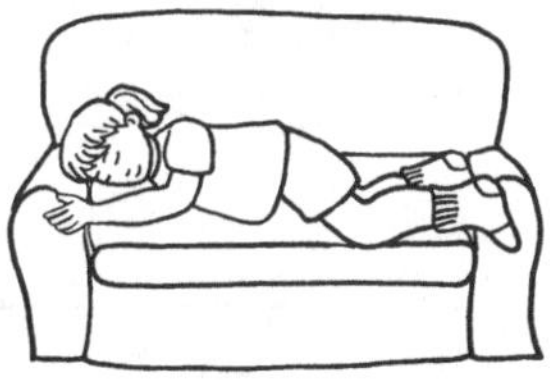

re

4.

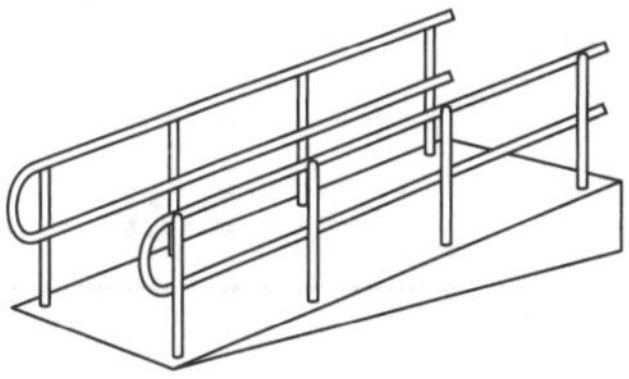

ra

5.

ju

6.

fa

Read It Together Jump and run fast. Then rest!

Name ______________________ Date ______________

Phonics

Ending -ed

Read the word. Add *-ed* and write the new word on the line. Read the sentence.

sprint

____

1. Pam ______________________ .

pass

____

2. She ______________________ it.

kick

____

3. Jess ______________________ .

jump

____

4. Hank ______________________ .

block

____

5. Hank ______________________ it.

Name ____________________ Date __________

Grammar & Writing

Write the Present Tense

1. **Read each word in the word box.**
2. **Read each sentence. Write the correct word on the line in each sentence.**
3. **Use each word only once.**

like	tell	read
washes	eats	mix

1. Sometimes, I mix pancakes for breakfast.
2. My sister ____________ cereal every morning.
3. My dogs ____________ a treat after their morning walk.
4. Mom and Dad sometimes ____________ the newspaper.
5. You never ____________ me what you want to eat.
6. My brother ____________ everyone's cups after we eat breakfast.

Name ______________________ Date ____________

Grammar: Present Tense Verbs

From Farm to Market

Grammar Rules **Present Tense Verbs**

Tell what one person or thing does now.	Use *s* at the end of the verb.
Marta sell*s* fruit.	

Read each sentence. Circle the correct word. Write the word.

1. The farm grows flowers. grow / grows
2. Leo and Rita ______ flowers. grow / grows
3. The woman ______ flowers. sell / sells
4. Kyle and Eva ______ flowers. sell / sells
5. Mom ______ flowers. buy / buys
6. Andy and Jorge ______ flowers. buy / buys

Make a list of verbs with a partner. Write a sentence with one verb for your partner to read aloud.

Name ______________________ Date ____________

Phonics

Words with ch, tch

chin

Circle the word that names the picture.
Read and answer the question.

1.

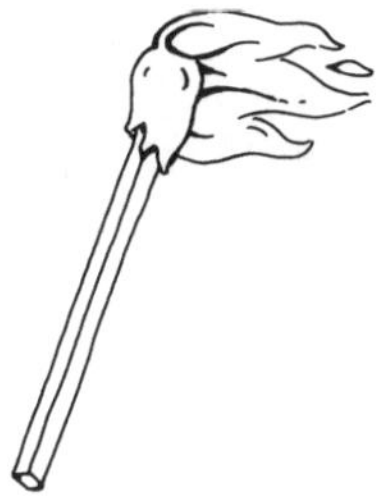

mask

mast

match

2.

chap

chest

catch

3.

batch

bash

bench

4.

past

pats

patch

5.

drink

chin

win

6.

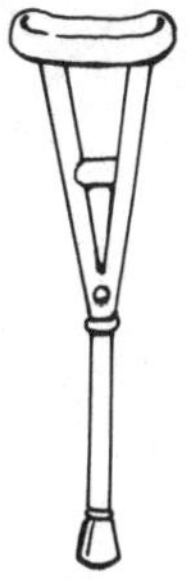

crutch

crust

club

Read It Together Do you put a patch on pants or a bench?

Name ____________________ Date ____________

Idea Web

Identify Details

Complete the Idea Web. Place one answer to the question in each circle.

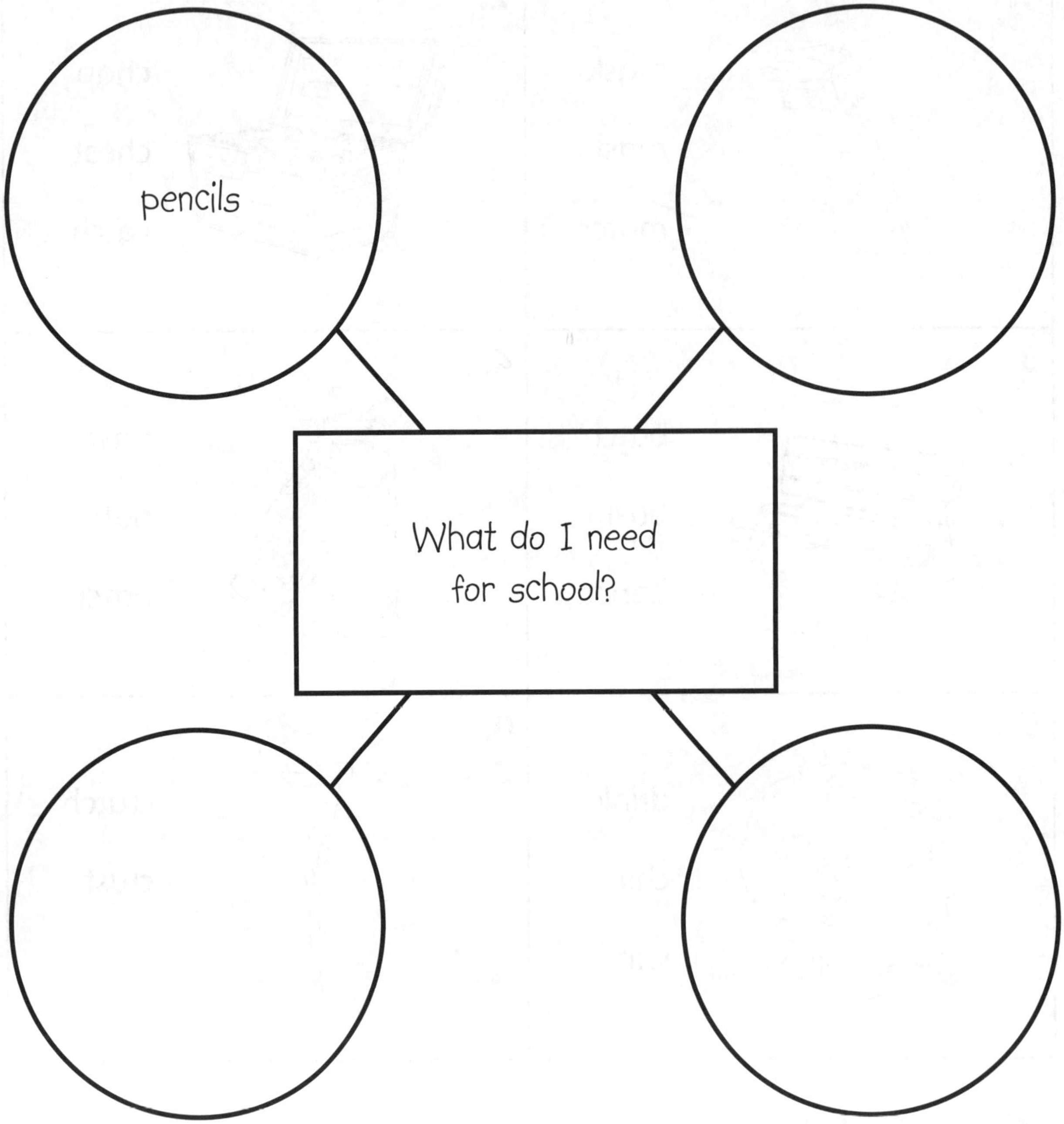

Name ______________________________ Date ______________

Grammar

Use *Am* and *Are*

1. Get a marker. Take turns with a partner.
2. Put your marker on a pronoun—**I**, **we**, or **you**.
3. Slide your marker to a verb—**am** or **are**.
4. Can you make a sentence? Get one point.
(Hint: I am ________ . We are ________ . You are ________ .)
5. Now your partner gets a turn.
6. Play until both partners make five sentences.

are	am	are	am	are	am
I	We	You	We	I	You

Name ______________________ Date ______________

Phonics

Words with ch, tch

Write the letters to complete the word. Read and answer the question.

1.

chain

2.

ick

3.

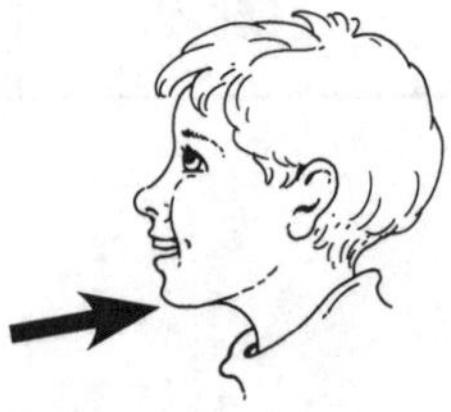

in

4.

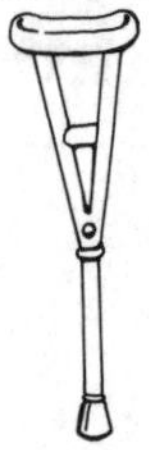

cru

5.

pea

6.

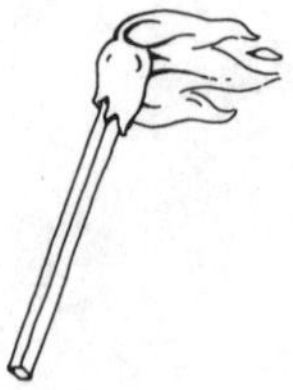

ma

Read It Together Can a chick sit on a bench?

Name ______________________ Date __________

Phonics

Blend Words

Circle the word that names the picture. Read and answer the question.

1.  brand (branch)	**2.**  chop plop	**3.** 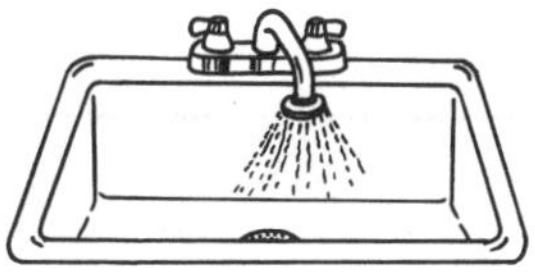 such sink
4.  spin chin	**5.**  ring rich	**6.** 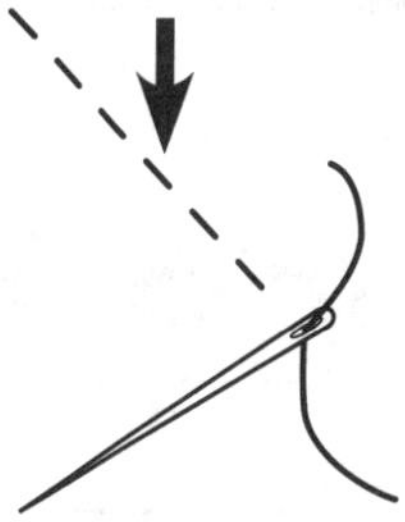 sting stitch
7. 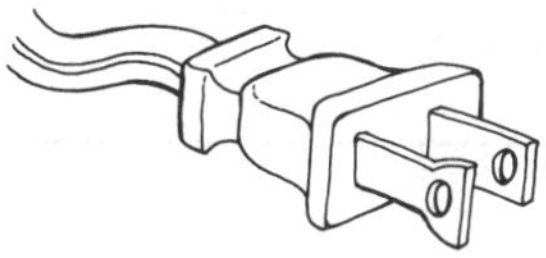 plug chug	**8.**  crunch crust	**9.** 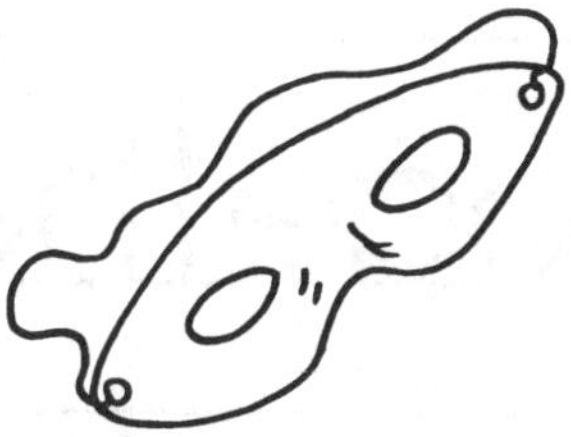 much mask

Read It Together How much of the branch will he chop up?

Name ______________________ Date ____________

Handwriting

High Frequency Words

Trace each word two times and then write it.

around around around

be be be

here here here

need need need

together together

together

where where where

Word Cards: *ch, tch, th*

 lunch	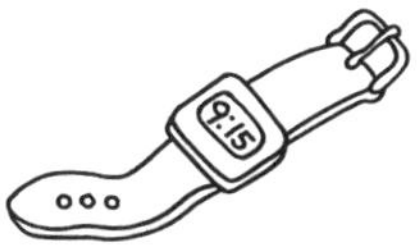 watch	 cloth	 chick
chop	thump	hatch	thick
thing	chill	ranch	that
pitch	check	catch	such
path	itch	patch	with
chest	rich	chat	witch
batch	chin	math	much

Spelling & Word Work

High Frequency Word Cards

does	around
eat	be
live	here
no	need
see	together
why	where

Name ______________________ Date ____________

Phonics

Words with th

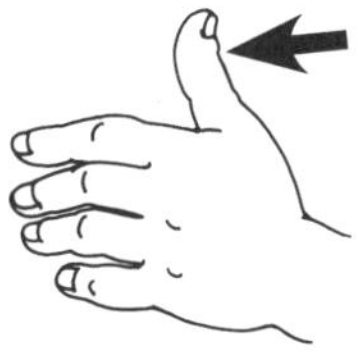

Circle the word that names the picture. Read the sentence.

1.

think

sink

drink

2.

chin

thin

tin

3.

pan

that

path

4.

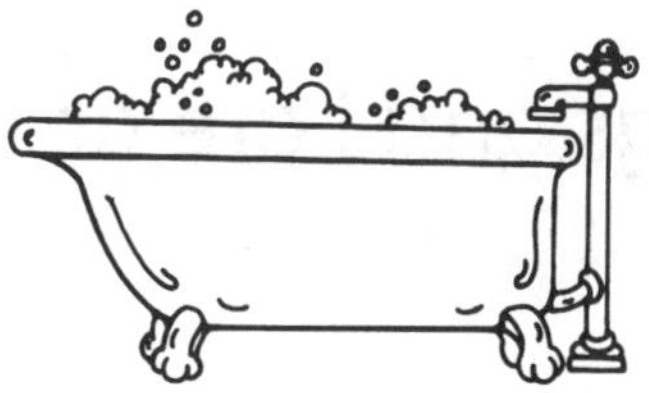

band

bath

bank

5.

then

test

tent

6.

tank

thank

than

Read It Together Thad can thank Ruth for this.

Name ______________________________ Date ______________

High Frequency Words

Fetch It!

Look at the picture. Write a word from the box to complete each sentence. Read the sentence.

High Frequency Words
around
be
here
need
together
where

1. My dogs and I are at the pond ______________ .

2. I toss a stick, and they ______________ to find it.

3. My dogs sniff all ______________ . They can not find the stick!

4. ______________ can the stick be?

5. Look! It is ______________ in the sand by the big rock!

Name ______________________ Date ____________

Phonics

Words with th

Write the letters to complete each word. Read and answer the questions.

1.

thimble

2.

____ink

3.

tee____

4.

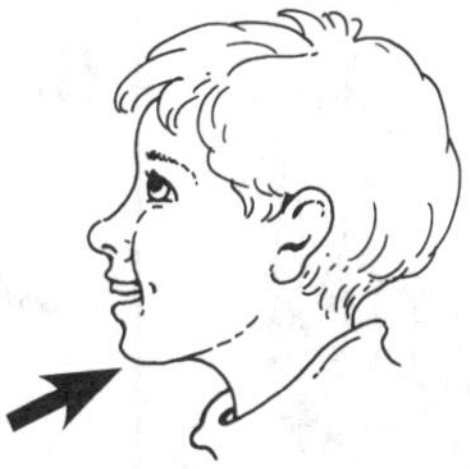

____in

5.

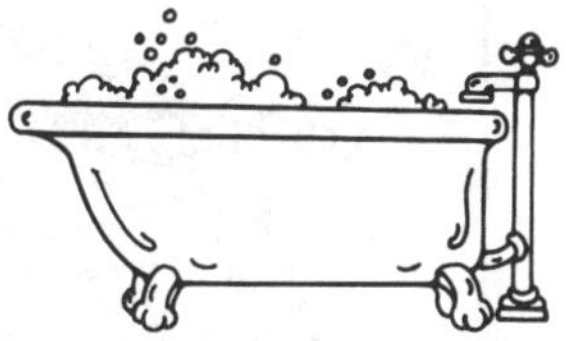

ba____

6.

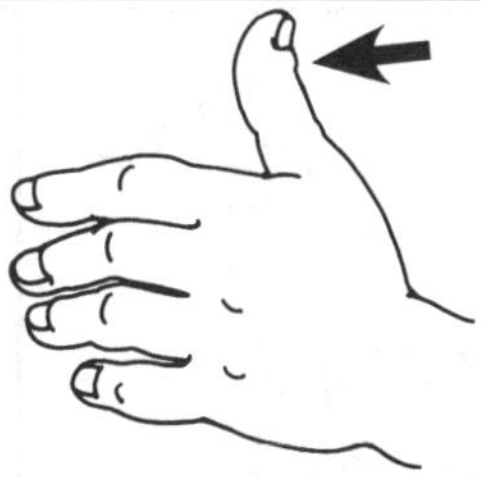

____umb

Read It Together Does a dog want a bath? What do you think?

Name ______________________ Date ____________

Phonics

Blend Words

Circle the word that names the picture. Read and answer the question.

1.  thick chick	**2.**  moth much	**3.**  thin chin
4.  chomp them	**5.**  math match	**6.** 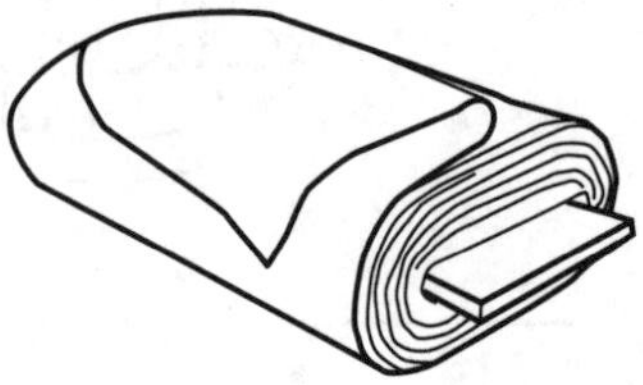 cloth clutch
7.  thump chump	**8.**  think chimp	**9.**  patch path

Read It Together Do you think that math is fun?

Name ______________________ Date ____________

Grammar and Writing

Be and the Present Progressive

1. Read the words in the box.
2. Then read the letter.
3. Write the words that correctly complete the sentences in the letter.
4. Use each word only once.

are sitting	is waving	are
is saying	am writing	is

Dear Uncle Nick,

I am writing to you today from summer camp. Camp ____________ a lot of fun. We work in the garden and learn about food every day. My best friends here ____________ Ann and Tess. Right now, we ____________ under a big tree near our cabin. Ann ____________ to you and Tess ____________ hello. See you soon.

Love,
Ella

Name ____________________ Date ____________

Vocabulary

Vocabulary Bingo

1. **Write Key Words on the lines.**
2. **Listen to the clues. Place a marker on the Key Word.**
3. **Say "Bingo" when you have four markers in a row.**

Name ______________________ Date ____________

Idea Web

Delivery

Complete the Idea Web using details from "Delivery."

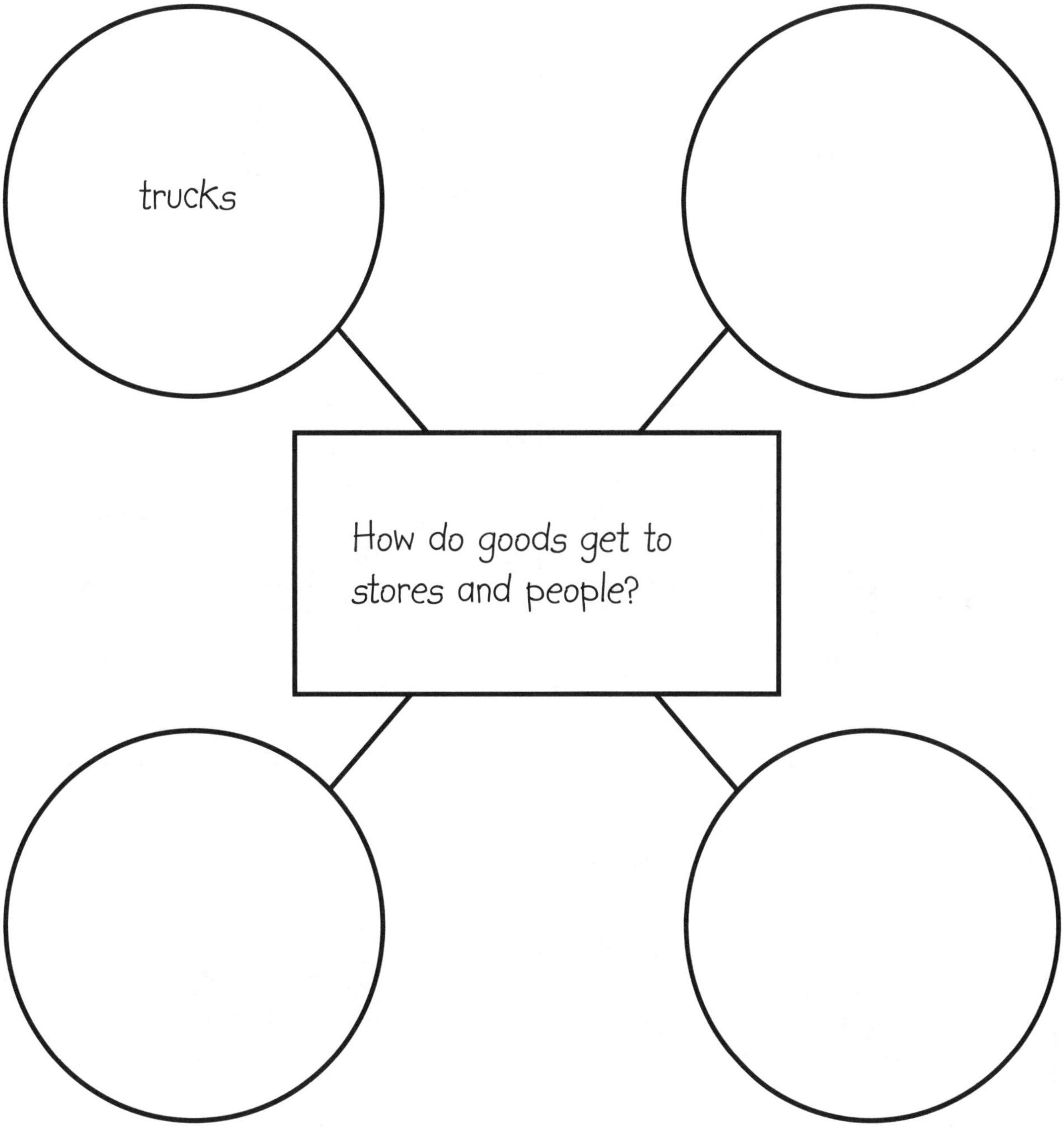

Use your Idea Web to retell the poem to a partner.

For use with TE p. T188

Name ______________________________ Date ______________

Phonics

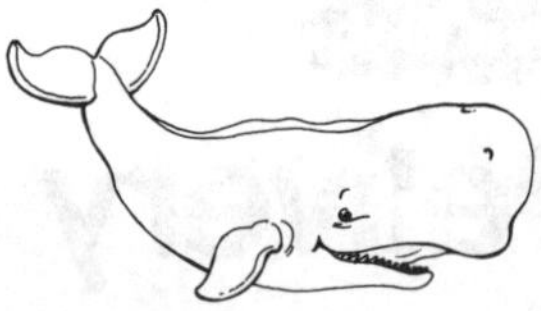

Words with wh

Circle the word that names the picture. Read and answer the question.

1.

thank

check

whack

2.

chin

when

thin

3.

whisk

thick

chuck

4.

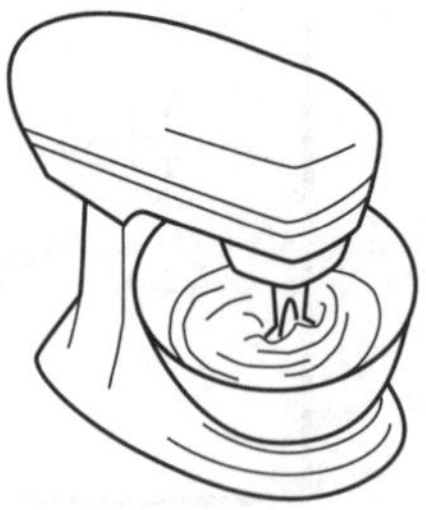

chip

whip

with

5.

which

chick

think

6.

whiff

cliff

fifth

Read It Together Do you use a whiff or a whisk when you mix?

Name ______________________ Date ____________

Phonics

Words with wh

Write the letters to complete the word. Read and answer the question.

1.

whip

2.

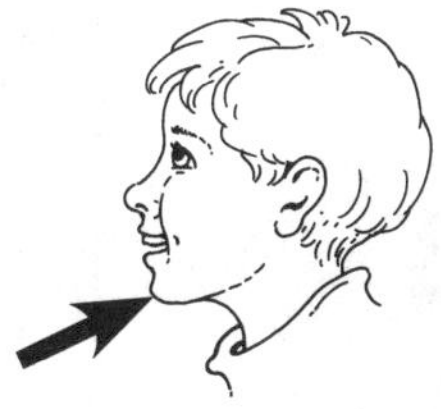

in

3.

ale

4.

iz

5.

ink

6.

eel

Read It Together What can you see whiz by when you go out?

Name ______________________ Date ____________

Phonics

Blend Words

Circle the word that names the picture. Read and answer the question.

1.  think whisk	**2.**  which chimp	**3.**  check what
4. 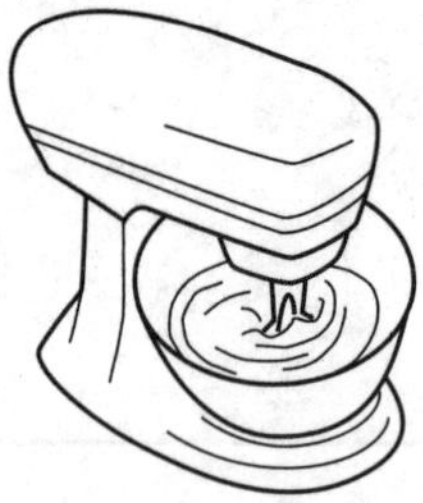 with whip	**5.**  thank when	**6.**  whim whiff
7.  wham chat	**8.**  whack wing	**9.**  chop whiz

Read It Together What can you whack with a bat?

Name ______________________ Date ____________

Handwriting

High Frequency Words

Trace each word two times and then write it.

come come come

found found found

full full full

next next next

their their their

walk walk walk

Spelling & Word Work

Word Cards: *wh, sh*

 whiff	 ship	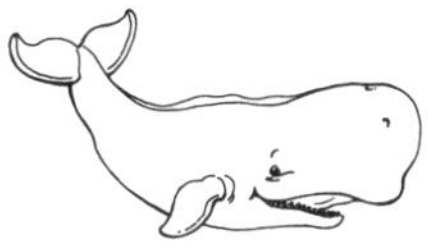 whale	 shell
shy	whisk	why	shack
should	shin	which	where
mush	whim	she	whip
when	shall	wash	whomp
shed	what	wham	shop
wheel	shawl	whiz	dish

Spelling & Word Work

High Frequency Word Cards

all	come
are	found
by	full
first	next
more	their
there	walk

Name ______________________ Date ____________

Respond and Extend: T-Chart

Compare Genres

Compare a poem and a fact sheet.

Poem	Fact Sheet
has illustrations or pictures	has photographs

Tell a partner how a poem and a fact sheet are different. Use your T-chart.

Name ______________________ Date ____________

Phonics

Words with sh

ship

Circle the word that names the picture. Read the tongue twister.

1.

shop
chip
sip

2.

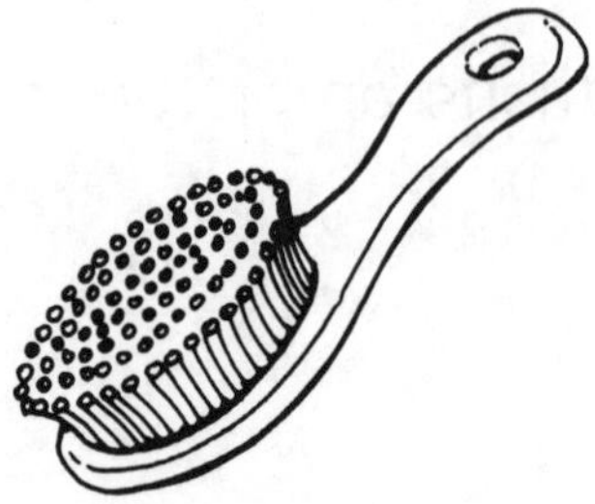

broth
brush
brick

3.

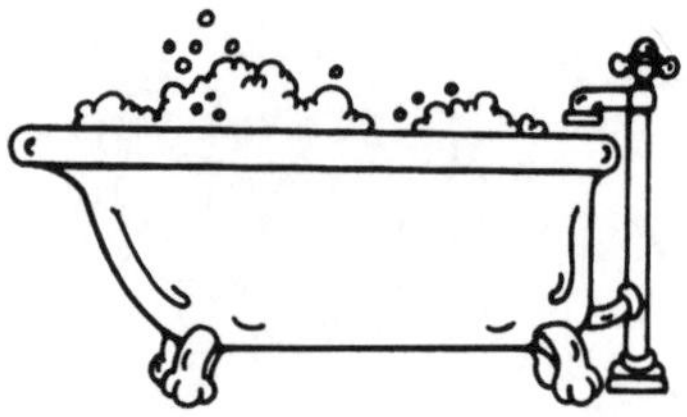

bash
bath
batch

4.

thud
when
shed

5.

shelf
whiff
self

6.

ditch
dust
dash

Read It Together She put shells on the shelf in the shop.

Name ______________________ Date ____________

High Frequency Words

What Did I Find?

Write a word from the box to complete each sentence. Guess the answer to the riddle.

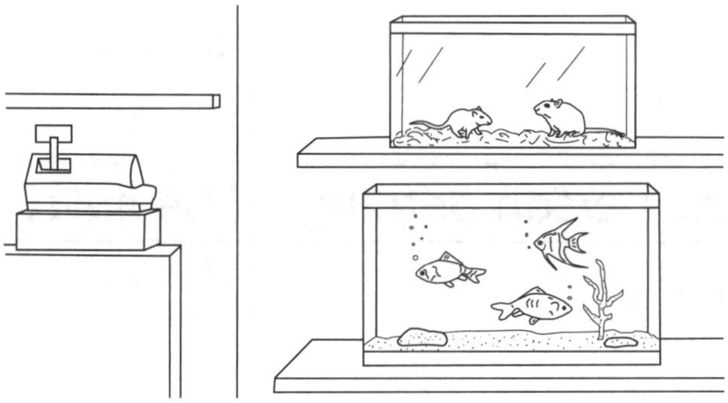

High Frequency Words
come
found
full
next
their
walk

1. Come and see what I ____________ in the shop!

2. They have no legs, but you can see ____________ fins.

3. They can swim, but they can not ____________ .

4. This tank is ____________ of them.

5. My ____________ pet will be one of them.
What are they?

Name ____________________ Date ____________

Grammar: Verb: *Have*

Use *Have* and *Has*

Grammar Rules Verbs: have

Some verbs tell what the subject of a sentence has.

Subject	*Have*
I, you, or more than one person or thing	Use *have.*
one other person or thing	Use *has.*

1. **Play One, Two, Three. Choose a word in Row 1.**
2. **Choose the verb that matches in Row 2.**
3. **Complete the sentence with a phrase from Row 3.**
4. **Take turns with a partner.**

Row 1			
Marcus	I	Julio and Sara	Karen
Row 2			
has	has	have	have
Row 3			
 a truck.	 a plane.	 a train.	 a van.

Read your sentences to a partner.

Name ______________________ Date ____________

Phonics

Words with sh

Write the letters to complete the word. Read the sentence.

1.

ship

2.

fi

3.

ick

4.

ell

5.

ain

6.

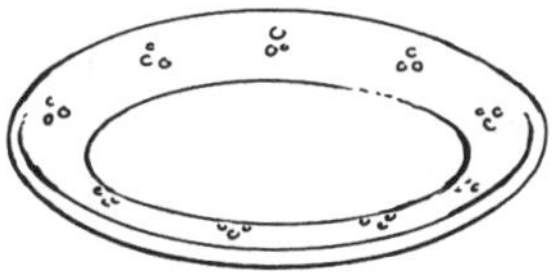

di

Read It Together See the fish swim around the shell!

Name ______________________________ Date ______________

Phonics

Blend Words

Circle the word that names the picture. Read and answer the question.

1.  shin chin	**2.**  brush brunch	**3.**  catch cash
4.  shack check	**5.**  such sash	**6.** 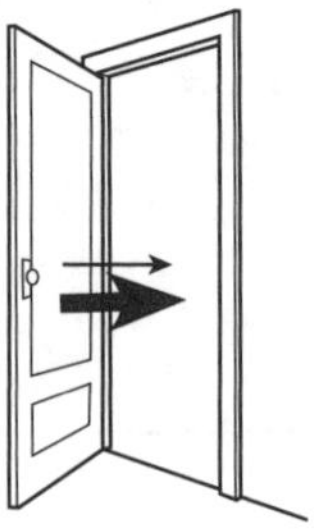 shut what
7. 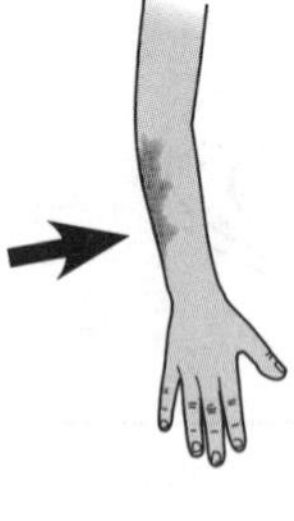 rash rich	**8.**  whip ship	**9.**  flash shelf

Read It Together What do you shop for when you have cash?

Name ______________________ Date ____________

Grammar & Writing

Write Forms of *Have* and *Be*

Present Tense Verbs		Contractions
has	**am**	**I'm**
have	**is**	**he's, she's, it's**
	are	**you're, they're**

Look at the paragraphs. Write the missing words in the blanks. Use words from the chart.

My uncle __is__ a farmer. He ____________ a huge tractor. ____________ as tall as my house!

Farmers ____________ hard workers. Sometimes ____________ up at 4 o'clock in the morning. ____________ glad I do not get up at 4 a.m.!

Name ______________________ Date ______________

Grammar: Subject-Verb Agreement

Who Is? Who Has?

Grammar Rules Subject-Verb Agreement

Subject	***To be***	***To have***
one person or thing	is	has
more than one person or thing	are	have

Look at each picture below. Choose the correct verb in ( ) and write it on the line.

1. This ____is____ Tim. (is, are)

2. Lara ____________ a cart. (have, has)

3. The children ____________ hungry. (is, are)

4. Max and Sue ____________ food. (have, has)

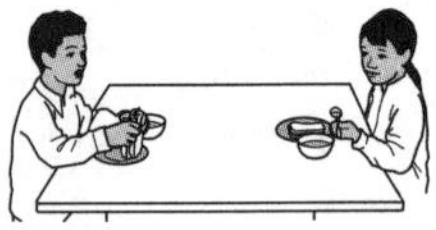

5. Max and Sue ____________ full. (am, are)

Choose a form of *be* or *have*. Ask a partner to say a sentence using it.

Name ______________________________ Date ______________

Prewrite Graphic Organizer: Idea Web

Idea Web

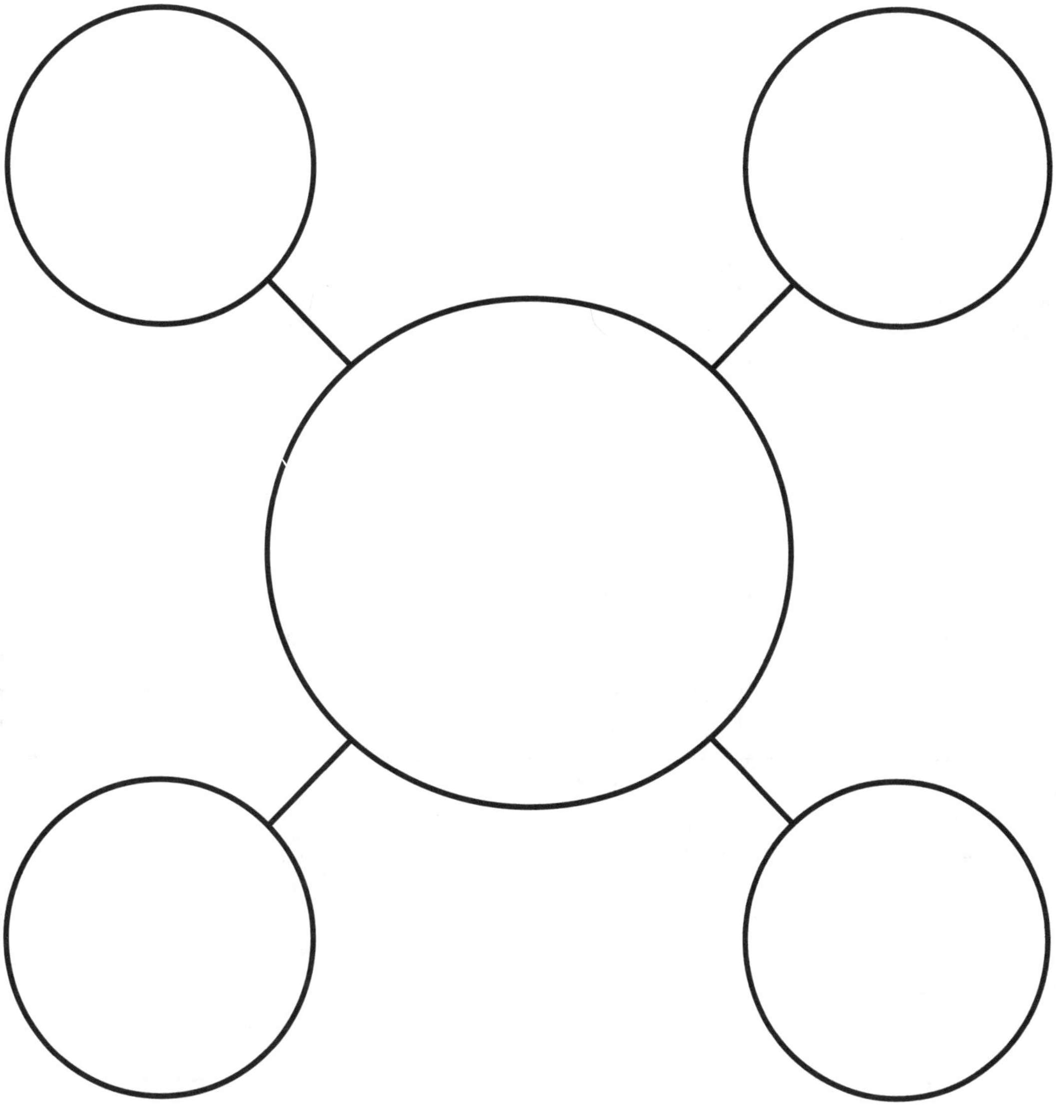

Voice Checklist

✓ Did you pick expressive words?
✓ Does your writing sound like you?
✓ Does your writing sound real?
✓ Do your words say what you want?

Name ____________________ Date ____________

Phonics

Words with Long a

cake

Circle the word that names each picture.

1.

rack
rake
rat

2.

lane
lamp
long

3.

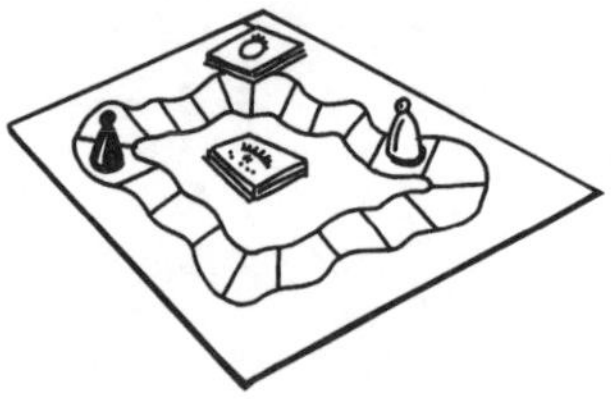

game
gas
gum

4.

bell
bake
bed

5.

cape
cat
cut

6.

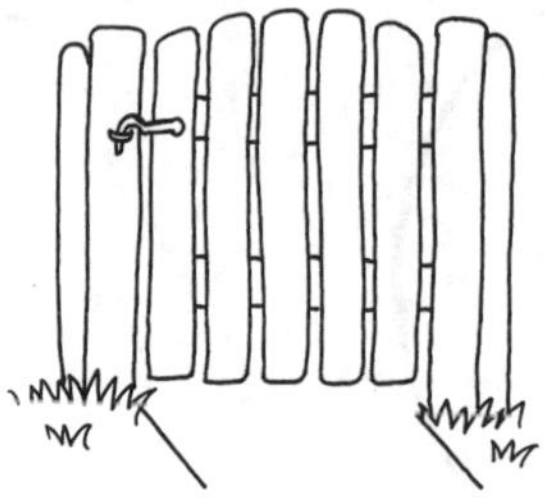

got
get
gate

7.

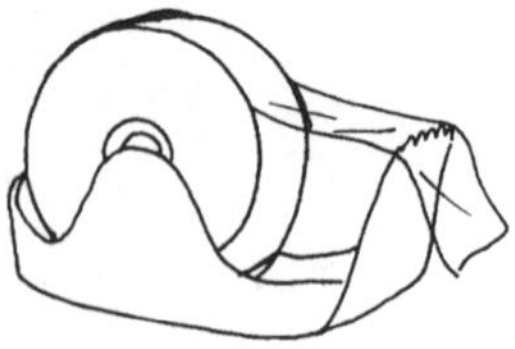

tap
tape
tack

8.

wave
wax
well

Read It Together Take the rake to the gate.

Name ______________________________ Date ______________

Beginning-Middle-End Chart

Identify Plot

Think of a story you know. Write or draw the plot in the chart.

Beginning:

Middle:

End:

Name ____________________ Date __________

Phonics

Blend Words

Circle the word that names each picture.

1.  cape cake	**2.** 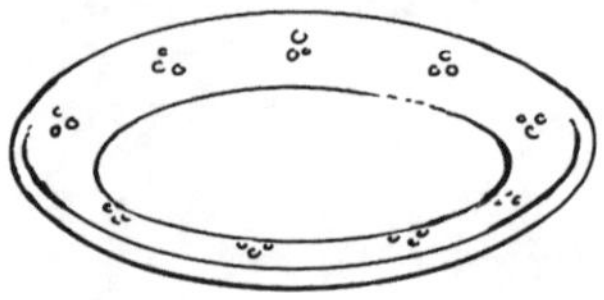 brake plate	**3.**  grape mane
4.  cane wave	**5.**  scale whale	**6.**  skate same
7.  date snake	**8.**  save flake	**9.**  frame plane

Read It Together Would a whale or a snake be in a lake?

Name ______________________ Date ____________

Phonics

Words with Long a

Complete each word so it names the picture.

1. 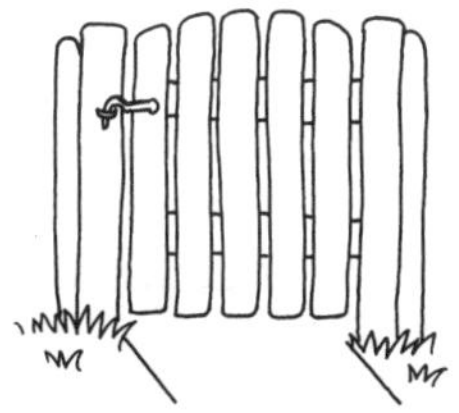 gate	**2.**  w v
3.  c k	**4.** 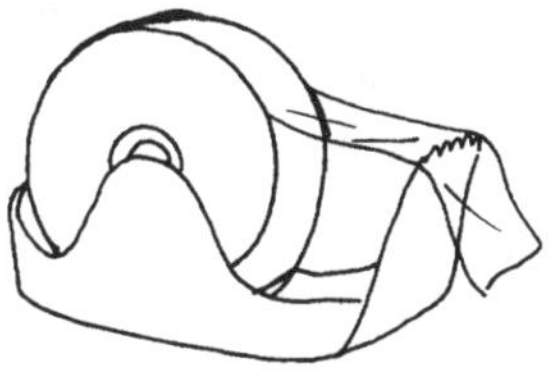 t p
5.  l k	**6.** 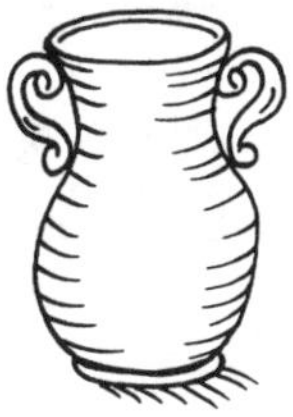 v s

Read It Together Look at the waves in the lake.

Name ______________________ Date ____________

Handwriting

High Frequency Words

Trace each word two times and then write it.

because because

because

carry carry carry

don't don't don't

new new new

play play play

sleep sleep sleep

Long a Word Cards

snake 	cane 	game 	gate 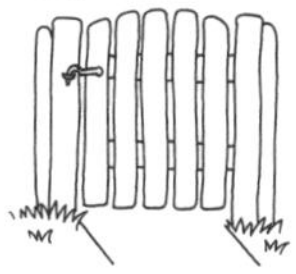
crate	bake	came	same
flame	cake	date	late
tame	wake	rake	mate
lane	lake	fame	rate
mane	flake	frame	plate
pane	take	plane	make

Spelling & Word Work

High Frequency Word Cards

go	because
great	carry
one	don't
saw	new
want	play
would	sleep

Name ______________________ Date ____________

Phonics

Contractions

what + is = what's	
is + not = isn't	

Read the sentences. Write the contraction for the underlined words.

1. Can you see what is in the pond?

   Can you see ______________ in the pond?

2. I can not see a cat in the pond.

   I ______________ see a cat in the pond.

3. It is not a cat.

   It ______________ a cat.

4. I think it is a fish!

   I think ______________ a fish!

Name ______________________ Date ____________

High Frequency Words

What's in the Box?

Write a word from the box to complete each sentence.

High Frequency Words
because
carry
don't
new
play
sleep

1. Jack and Beth ____________ have a dog.

2. They ____________ with Gramps's dog.

3. They help Gramps ____________ a box because it is big.

4. What's in the box? A ____________ pup is in it!

5. They will play. Then the pup will ____________.

Word Cards: Subject Pronouns

I	you	he	she
it	we	you *(more than one)*	they
duck	Dad	you and your sister	Dave
eggs	Ali and I	Mom	pond
my cousins and I	duckling	desk	myself
pencils	you and your brothers	Ana	yourself

Name ______________________ Date ____________

Phonics

Contractions

she	+ is	= she's
did	+ not	= didn't

Read the sentences. Write the contraction for the underlined words.

1. I did not see Jane. Did you?

I ________________ see Jane. Did you?

2. She is on the track.

________________ on the track.

3. Jake was not on the track.

Jake ________________ on the track.

4. I think he is at bat.

I think ________________ at bat.

Name ______________________________ Date ____________

Grammar and Writing

Write Subject Pronouns

One	More Than One
I	**we**
you	**you**
he (for a male)	**they**
she (for a female)	**they**
it (for a thing or place)	**they**

Look at each pair of sentences. Look at the underlined words in the first sentence. Write the correct pronoun in the second sentence.

1. Maya and Janet look at the ducklings. ________ look at them every day.

2. Maya feeds the ducklings. ________ feeds them bread.

3. Richard walks around the pond. ________ walks quickly.

4. The pond is big. ________ is the ducks' home. [anno:] It

5. My friend and I watch the ducklings, too. ________ are happy to see them grow.

6. You and your sister must be quiet! ________ might scare the ducklings away.

Name ______________________________ Date ______________

Vocabulary

Vocabulary Bingo

1. Write a Key Word in each egg.
2. Listen to the clues. Place a marker on the Key Word.
3. Say "Bingo" when you have four markers in a row.

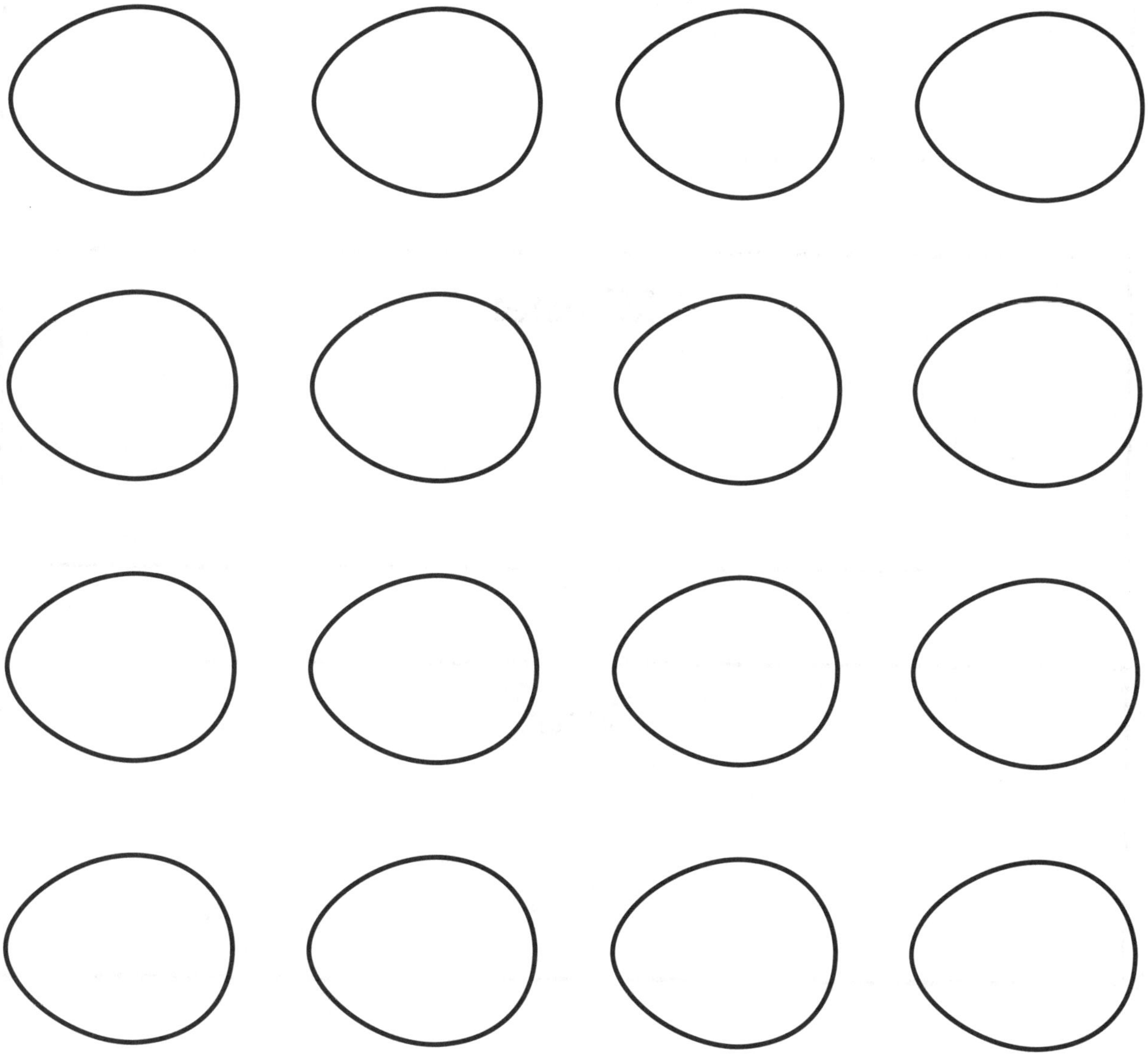

Name ______________________ Date ____________

Beginning-Middle-End Chart

Ruby in Her Own Time

Complete the chart. Write the important parts of the plot from the story.

Beginning:
First, Ruby hatches from an egg.

Middle:

End:

Use your chart to retell the story. Act out the events in order to a partner.

Name ______________________ Date ____________

Phonics

Words with Long i

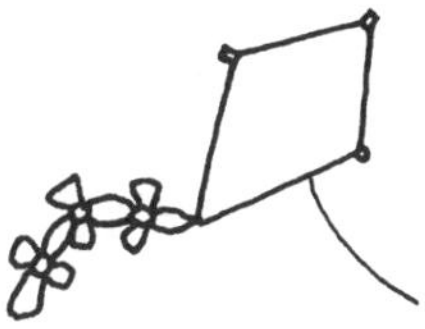

kite

Circle the word that names each picture.

1. 
fin
fan
five

2. 
back
bake
bike

3. 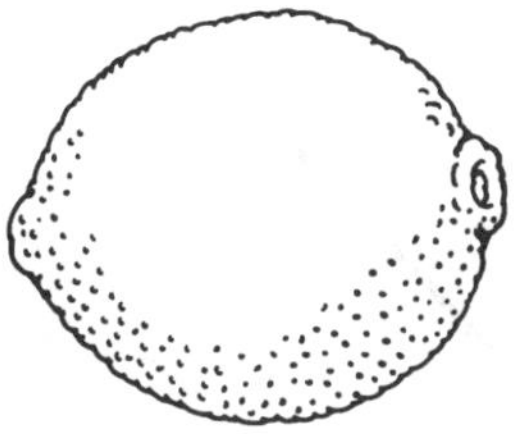
lime
lip
lamp

4. 
dive
date
desk

5. 

date
dime
dim

6. 
name
nine
nest

7. 
him
hale
hive

8. 
bite
bib
brake

Read It Together Would you like five dimes or five limes?

Name ______________________________ Date ______________

Grammar

The Pronoun Game

1. **Make a spinner.**
2. **Play with a partner.**
3. **Take turns spinning the spinner.**
4. **Say a sentence with the pronoun.**

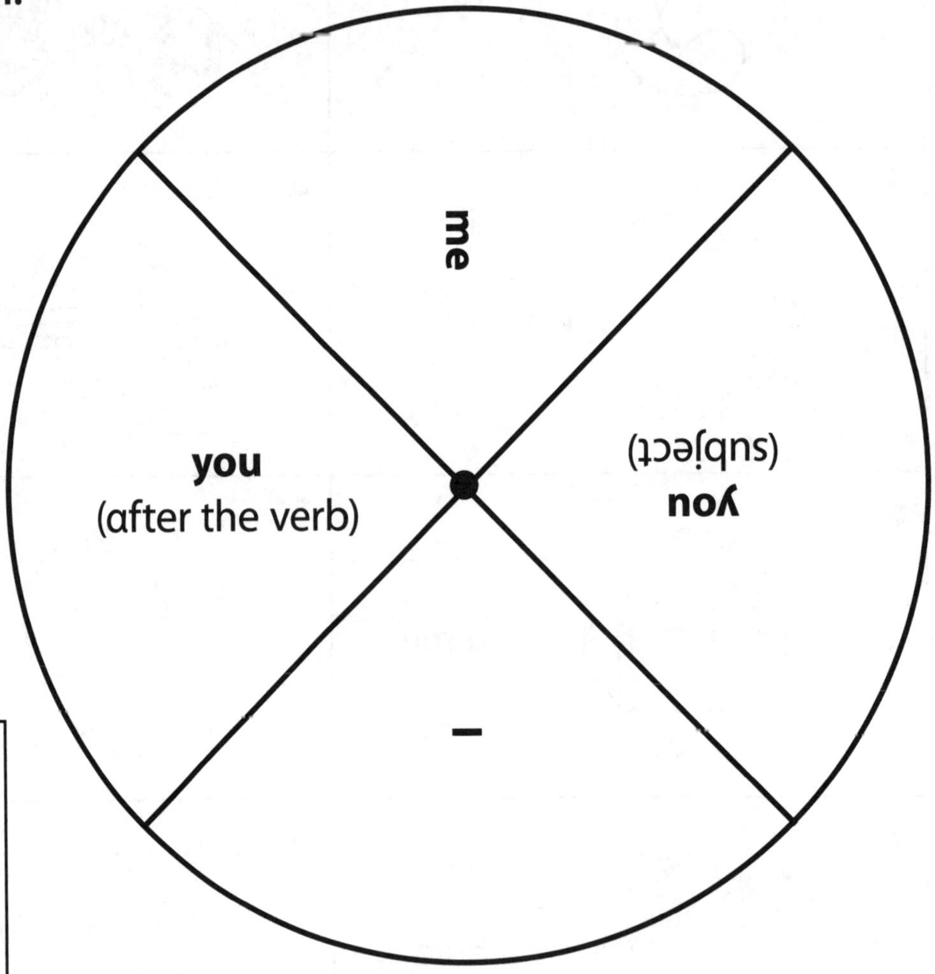

Make a Spinner

1. Put a paper clip in the center of the circle.
2. Hold one end of the paper clip with a pencil.
3. Spin the paper clip around the pencil.

Name ______________________ Date ____________

Phonics

Blend Words

Circle the word that names the picture.

1. 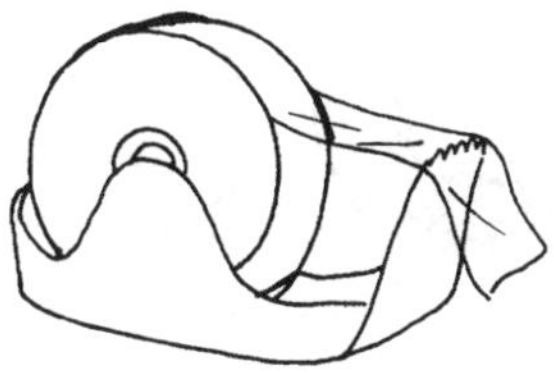 tap tape	**2.**  rid ride	**3.**  can cane
4. 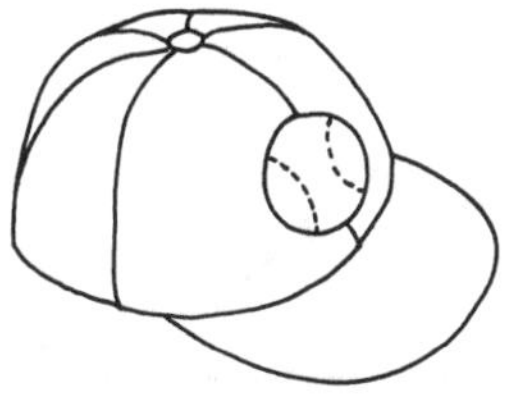 cap cape	**5.**  dim dime	**6.**  pin pine
7.  hat hate	**8.** 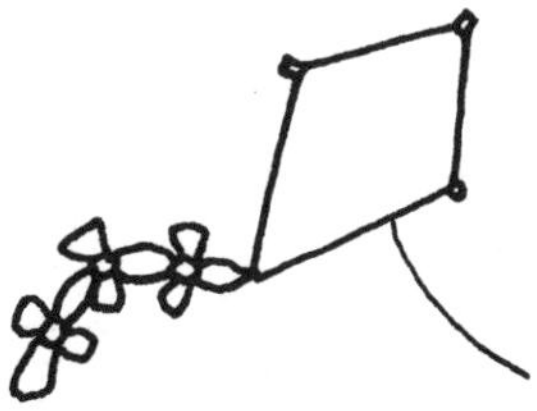 kit kite	**9.**  man mane

Read It Together Can a man ride a kite or a bike?

Name ______________________ Date ______________

Phonics

Words with Long i

Complete each word so it names the picture.

1.

dime

2.

d t

3.

f v

4.

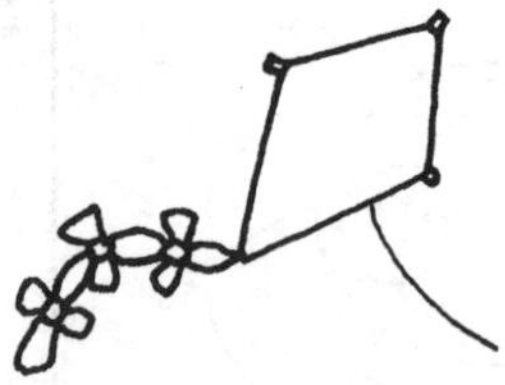

k t

5.

v s

6.

h v

Read It Together Give me the kite and five dimes.

Name ______________________ Date ____________

Handwriting

High Frequency Words

Trace each word two times and then write it.

almost almost almost

both both both

kind kind kind

over over over

two two two

was was was

Spelling & Word Work

Long i Word Cards

bride 	pile 	time 	five 
smile	slide	dive	slide
mime	stride	hive	slime
hide	glide	hide	dime
file	tile	tide	thrive
wide	side	ride	strive
while	lime	drive	mile

Spelling & Word Work

High Frequency Word Cards

give	almost
he	both
know	kind
said	over
watch	two
who	was

Name ______________________ Date ______________

Venn Diagram

Compare Genres

Compare a story and a science article.

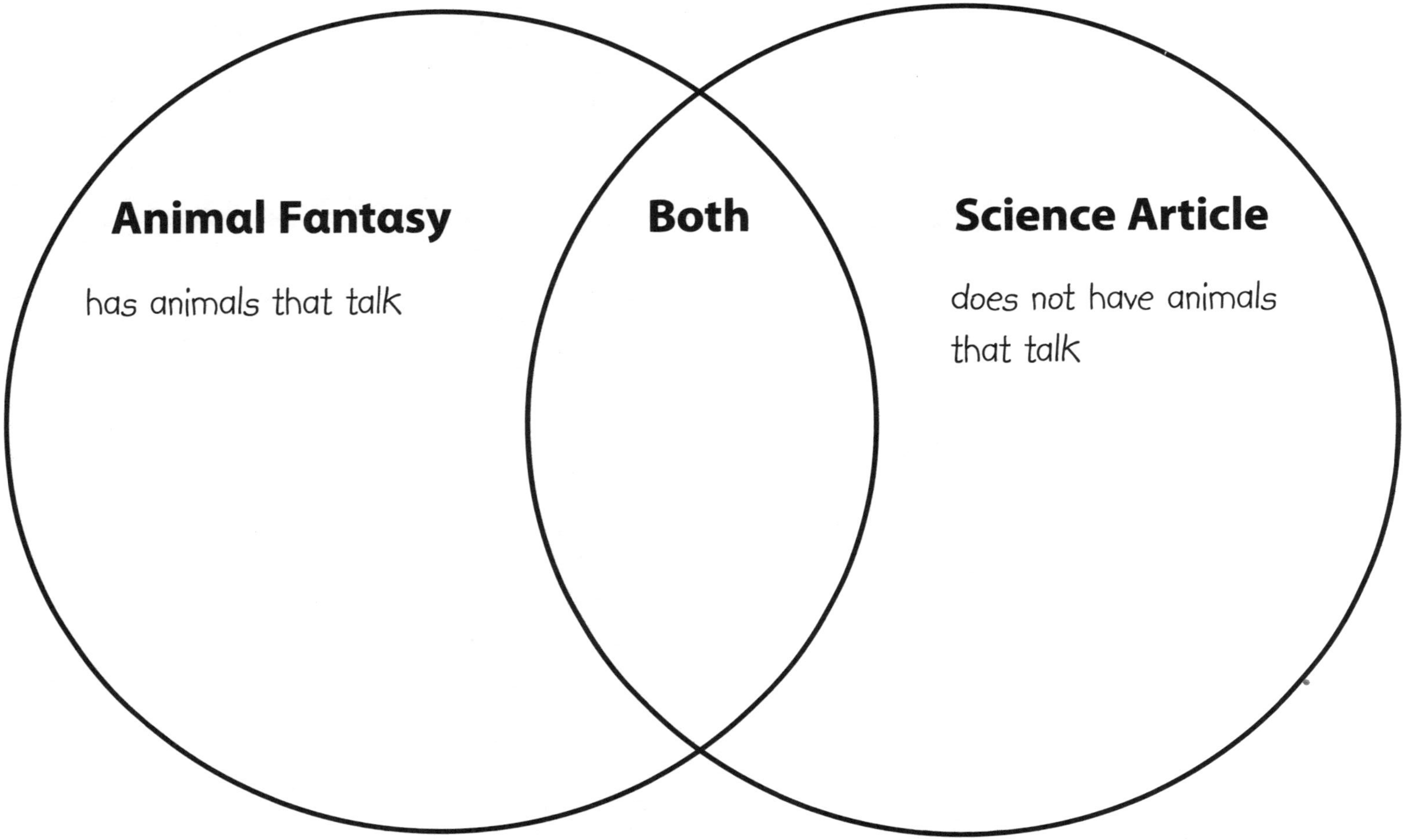

Tell a partner how a story and a science article are different. Then tell how they are the same.

Grammar

Word Cards

me	you	him
her	it	them
turtle	Dad	Paul
eggs	ocean	Mom
egg	nests	yourself
turtles	myself	Mara

Name ______________________ Date ____________

Phonics

Ending -ed

grin	+ n	+ ed	=	grinned
bake	– e	+ ed	=	baked

Add the ending *-ed* to each word and write the new word.

grin

1. He ______________________.

bake

2. He ______________________.

clap

3. She ______________________.

smile

4. He ______________________.

Name ______________________________ Date ______________

Phonics

Ending -ing

run	+ n	+ ing	=	running
bake	– e	+ ing	=	baking

Add the ending *-ing* to each word and write the new word.

jog

____

1. He is ______________________ .

dive

____

2. She is ______________________ .

swim

____

3. She is ______________________ .

wave

____

4. He is ______________________ .

Name ______________________ Date __________

High Frequency Words

At Bat

Write a word from the box to complete each sentence.

High Frequency Words
almost
both
kind
over
two
was

1. Stan ______________ at bat.

2. He had ______________ strikes.

3. The pitch came. It was the ______________ Stan liked.

4. He hit it up ______________ all the kids and almost out!

5. ______________ Mom and Dad clapped.

Name ______________________ Date ______________

Grammar and Writing

Write Pronouns

Subject	After the Verb
I	me
you	you
he	him
she	her
it	it
they	them

Look at each pair of sentences. Look at the underlined words in the first sentence. Write the correct pronoun in the second sentence.

1. Dave, Joe, and Ana watch the turtles. They watch them every day.
2. Dave, Joe, and Ana want to help them. ________ decide to feed them.
3. Dave feeds one turtle. He feeds ________ too much.
4. Joe meets Dave on the beach. ________ meets ________ at 4 p.m.
5. Joe sees Ana on the beach. He sees ________ on the sand.
6. I can't use all the turtle food. Please don't give ________ any more.

Name ____________________ Date __________

Phonics

Ending -ed

Circle the word that completes each sentence and write it.

hugged **hiked**

1. Zane ____________ up the path.

lugged **liked**

2. He ____________ to sing.

hummed **hated**

3. He ____________ a song as he walked.

jogged **jabbed**

4. Jen ____________ by Zane.

chopped **chimed**

5. She ____________ in and sang with him.

Name ______________________ Date ____________

Phonics

Ending -ing

Circle the word that completes each sentence and write it.

shopping **shining**

1. The sun is ____________ .

robbing **riding**

2. Shane is ____________ his bike on the path.

running **raking**

3. Meg is ____________ next to him.

chopping **chasing**

4. Matt is ____________ them on his skates.

stopping **sliding**

5. Are the pals ____________ to have a snack?

Name ______________________ Date ____________

Grammar

The Make-It-a-Pronoun Game

Grammar Rules Subject Pronouns

Use *I* for yourself.	I draw a turtle.
Use *he* for a male.	Jun draws a turtle. He draws a turtle
Use *she* for a female.	Aida draws a turtle. She draws a turtle.
Use *they* for more than one person.	Jun and Aida draw turtles. They draw turtles.

1. **Play with a partner.**
2. **Spin the spinner.**
3. **Change the noun to a subject pronoun.**

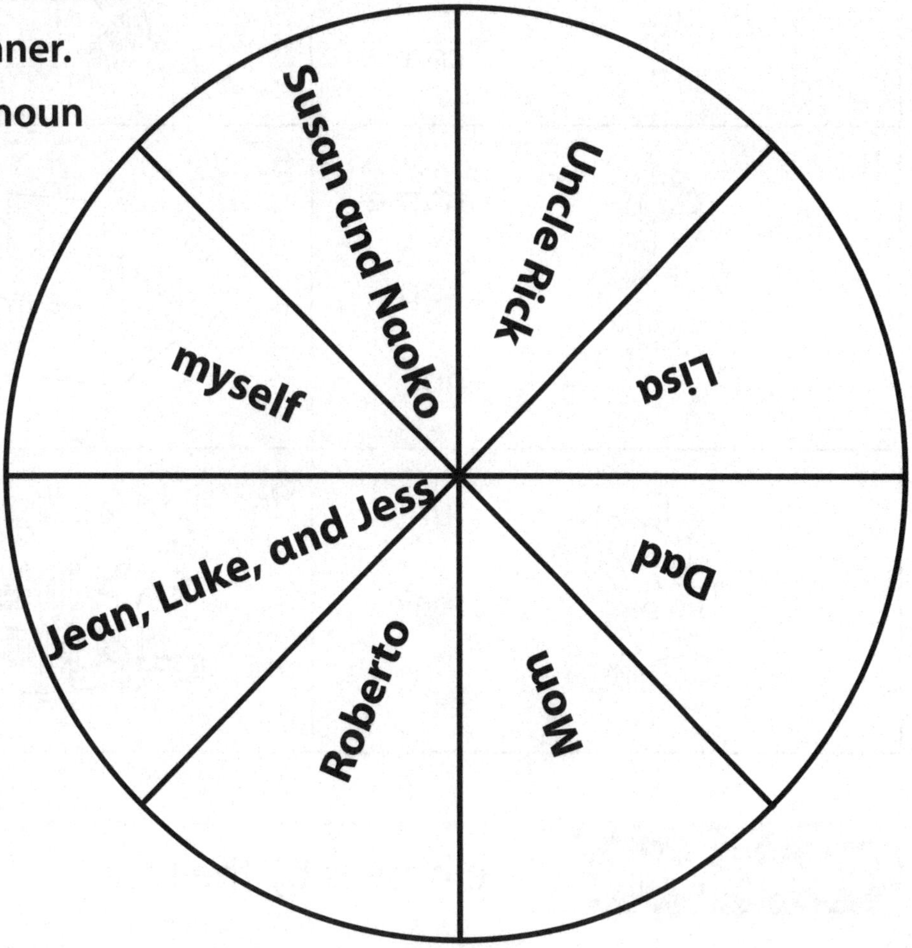

Make a Spinner

1. Put a paper clip in the center of the circle.
2. Hold one end of the paper clip with a pencil.
3. Spin the paper clip around the pencil.

Name ______________________ Date ____________

Phonics

Words with Long o

rope

Circle the word that names each picture.

1. 
   not
   nose
   name

2. 
   hate
   hat
   hose

3. 
   cone
   cane
   can

4. 
   rake
   rack
   robe

5. 

   name
   nap
   not

6. 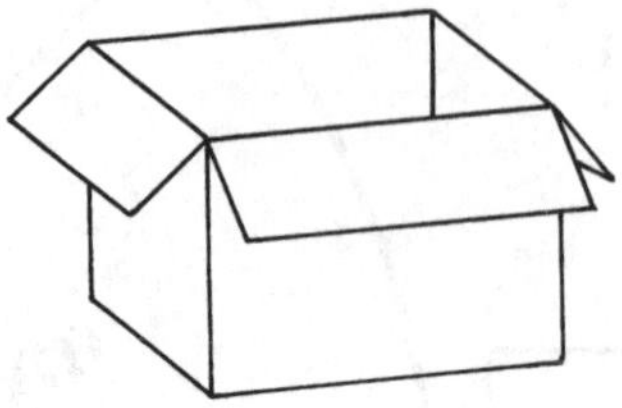
   box
   bone
   band

7. 
   run
   rock
   rose

8. 
   hot
   home
   hand

Read It Together The hose is by the roses at home.

Name ______________________ Date __________

Main Idea and Details Chart

Identify Main Idea and Details

Choose an animal. Write details about how the animal changes as it grows.

Main Idea: ______________________ change as they grow.
Detail:
Detail:
Detail:

Name ________________________ Date ____________

Phonics

Words with Long o

Complete each word so it names the picture.

1.  note	**2.**  c n
3. 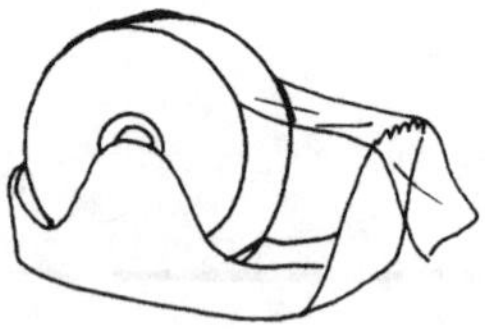 t p	**4.**  r s
5.  n s	**6.**  v s

Read It Together Smell the rose with your nose.

Name ______________________________ Date ____________

Phonics

Words with ph

phone

Complete each word so it names the picture.

1.  photo	**2.** 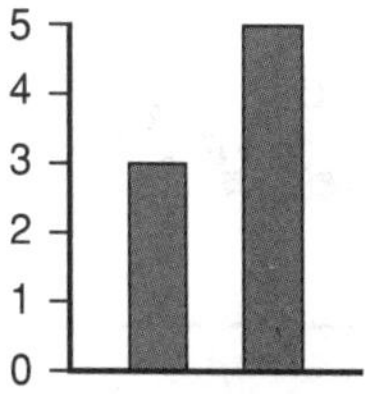 gra
3.  ink	**4.** 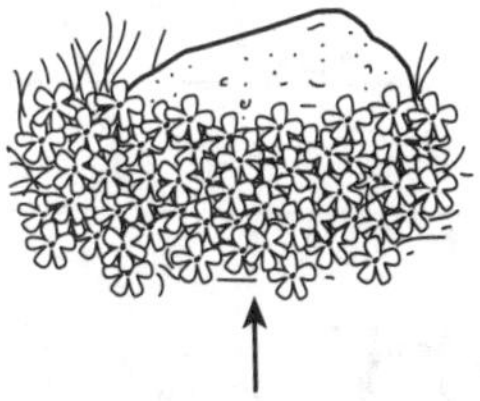 lox
5.  one	**6.** 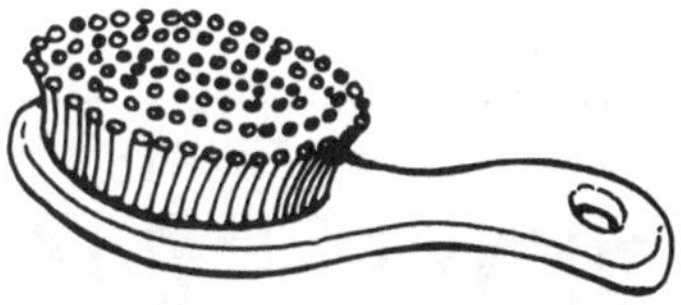 bru

Read It Together Would you see a graph or phlox by the rocks?

Name ______________________ Date ____________

Handwriting

High Frequency Words

Trace each High Frequency Word two times and then write it.

always always always

any any any

each each each

every every every

many many many

never never never

Spelling & Word Work

Long o Word Cards

cold 	hole 	bone 	hose 
nose	cone	gold	hold
close	pole	stone	phone
sold	rose	mold	bold
stole	pose	zone	mole
fold	role	shone	those
told	whole	lone	zone

Spelling & Word Work

High Frequency Word Cards

around	always
be	any
here	each
need	every
together	many
where	never

Name ______________________ Date ____________

Phonics

More Words with Long o

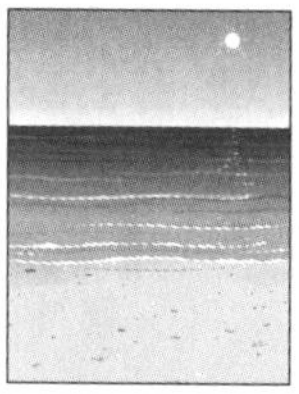

Complete each word so it names the picture.

1.  no	2.  ph n
3.  c k	4. 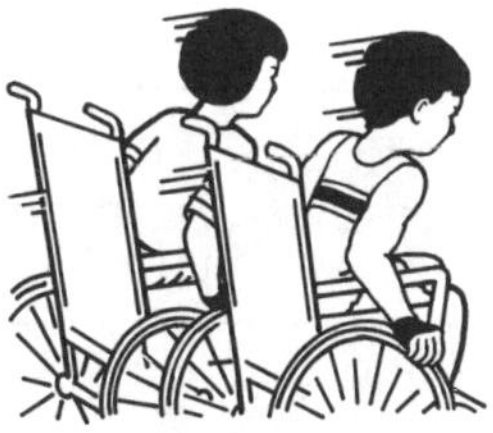 g
5.  pr	6.  J

Read It Together Jo wants to go see the pro play.

Name ______________________ Date ____________

High Frequency Words

Do You Have a Pet?

Write a word from the box to complete each sentence.

High Frequency **Words**
always
any
each
every
many
never

1. How ______________ kids in each class have pets?

2. We went to ______________ class and asked.

3. We ______________ asked kids with pets to stand.

4. Did ______________ class not have pets?

5. No. We ______________ found a class with no pets!

Name ________________________ Date ____________

Grammar

Word Sort: Possessive Nouns

1. Read each word in the top boxes.
2. Decide whether the word names one owner or more than one owner.
3. Write the word in the correct column of the chart.
4. Once all the words have been sorted, take turns using each one in a sentence.

girls'	**spider's**	**butterfly's**	**chicks'**
eggs'	**Mario's**	**baby's**	**cocoons'**

One Owner	More Than One Owner

Name ______________________ Date ____________

Phonics

More Words with Long o

Circle the word that completes each sentence and write it.

so **stove**

1. My dog is ____________ big!

Bo **nose**

2. He's white with a black ____________.

go **got**

3. He can ____________ very fast.

No **Note**

4. But he stops when I say, "____________."

pro **phone**

5. I am a ____________ with my big dog!

Name ______________________ Date __________

Grammar and Writing

Write Possessive Nouns

One Owner	More Than One Owner
boy's	**boys'**
cat's	**cats'**
egg's	**eggs'**
caterpillar's	**caterpillars'**

Look at each pair of sentences. Look at the underlined words in the first sentence. Write the correct pronoun in the second sentence.

1. The house of John has a big backyard. ________ house has a big backyard.

2. We see the nests of the birds in the tree. We see ________ nests in the tree.

3. The branches of the tree protect the nests. The ________ branches protect the nests.

4. The shells of the eggs are thin but strong. The ________ shells are thin but strong.

5. Are the eggs of the bird ready to hatch? Are the ________ eggs ready to hatch?

6. The beak of the baby pokes through the egg. The ________ beak pokes through the egg.

Name ______________________________ Date ______________

Vocabulary

Yes or No?

1. Listen to the questions. Write the Key Word where it belongs in each sentence.
2. Listen to the questions again.
3. Check *yes* or *no* for each question.

	yes	no
1. Can a ______________ hang from a leaf?	☐	☐
2. Does a ______________ stay the same as it grows?	☐	☐
3. Can a ______________ fly?	☐	☐
4. Does a ______________ lay eggs?	☐	☐
5. Does every ______________ have wings?	☐	☐
6. Will you ______________ as you grow?	☐	☐

Name ______________________ Date __________

Main Idea and Details Chart

A Butterfly is Born

Write details in the chart that tell how a caterpillar changes into a butterfly.

Main Idea: A caterpillar changes into a butterfly.
Detail: hatches from an egg
Detail:
Detail:
Detail:
Detail:
Detail:

Summarize what you learned about a butterfly's life to a partner. Use your Main Idea and Details Chart.

Name ______________________ Date ____________

Phonics

Words with u_e

Circle the word that names each picture.

cube

tube

1.

mile

mole

mule

2.

June

just

jab

3.

rude

ride

rid

4.

fit

flat

flute

5.

cab

cube

cub

6.

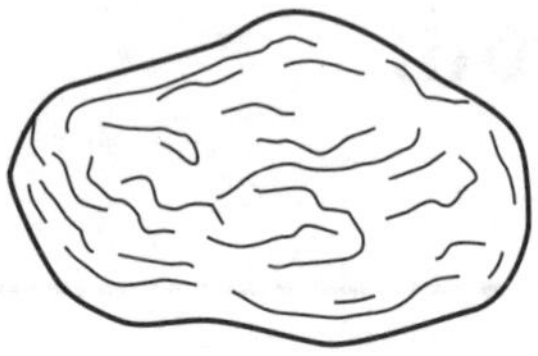

prune

pane

pine

7.

dine

dune

den

8.

ten

tine

tune

Read It Together Do you use a flute or a mule to play a tune?

Name ______________________ Date ____________

Phonics

Words with u_e

Complete each word so it names the picture.

1.

cube

2.

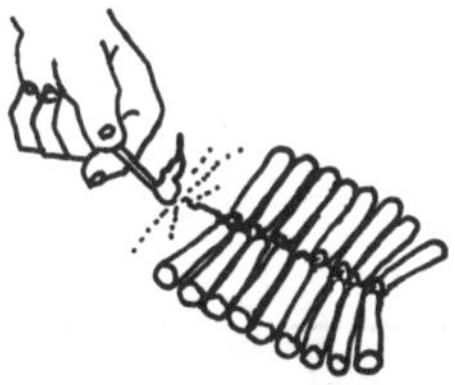

f s

3.

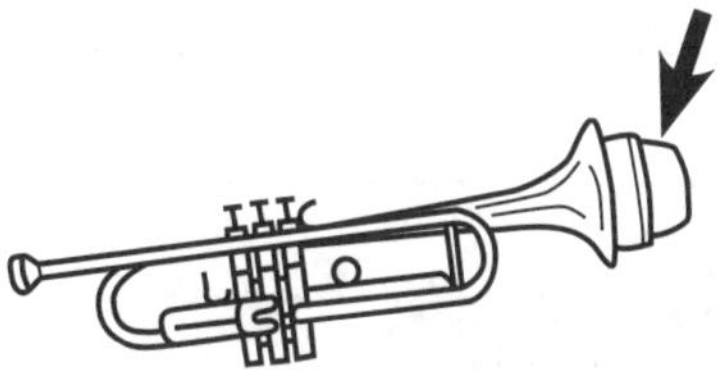

m t

4.

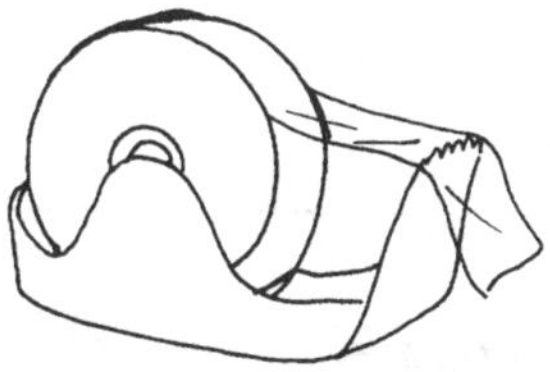

t p

5.

m l

6.

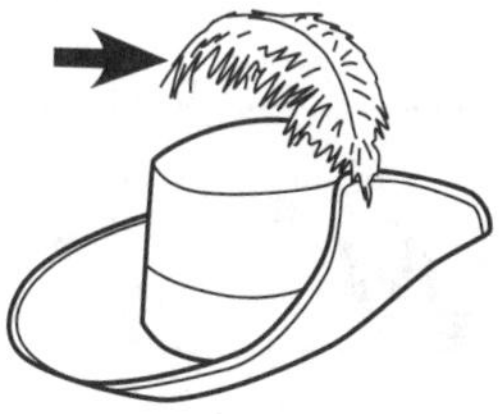

pl m

Read It Together Does a block look like a fuse or a cube?

Name ______________________ Date ____________

Handwriting

High Frequency Words

Trace each word two times and then write it.

four four four

may may may

only only only

other other other

show show show

some some some

Spelling & Word Work

Long u and Long e Word Cards

glue 	meat 	three 	fruit 
feel	suit	rescue	street
please	cute	these	tube
use	leaves	bean	huge
clue	peek	sneeze	teach
mule	due	flea	yeast
true	plume	beam	flute

Spelling & Word Work

High Frequency Word Cards

come	four
found	may
full	only
next	other
their	show
walk	some

Name ______________________ Date ____________

T-chart

Compare Genres

Compare a science article and a poem.

Science Article	Poem
has real information	has information that is not real

Tell a partner how a science article and a poem are different.

Name ______________________ Date ____________

Phonics

Words with Long e

Complete each word so it names the picture.

1.

he

2.

n

3.

sh

4.

w

5.

St v

6.

pr

Read It Together He is Steve, and she is Eve.

Name ______________________ Date ____________

High Frequency Words

Math Time

Write a word from the box to complete each sentence.

High Frequency Words
four
may
only
other
show
some

1. I will ______________ you some math.

2. Look! Two plus two is ______________ .

3. Here is some ______________ math.

4. You have two plums. ______________ I have one?

5. Now you have ______________ one plum, but I have one, too!

Name ______________________ Date ____________

Grammar

Who Owns It?

1. **Toss a marker onto one of the sentence parts below.**
2. **Put it together with another sentence part. The noun or pronoun should match the possessive word.**
3. **Write the complete sentence on a separate piece of paper.**
4. **Say the sentence to your partner.**

We	spreads its wings.
watches her caterpillar.	I
Maria	crawl on our knees.
They	Juan and I
uses his hand lens.	take care of your chrysalis.
The butterfly	explore our backyard.
climbs the tree to find its food.	You
read my insect books.	lives in its habitat.
Maria and Juan	record their findings.
They	The caterpillar

Name ______________________ Date ____________

Phonics

Words with Long e

Circle the word that completes each sentence and write it.

be **Pete**

1. My best pal is ______________ .

We **Theme**

2. ______________ play tunes together.

she **these**

3. I play ______________ drums.

He **Here**

4. ______________ plays that flute.

be **Steve**

5. Will you ______________ in a band with us?

Name ______________________ Date ____________

Phonics

Blend Words

Circle the word that names each picture.

1.  not note	**2.**  hop hope	**3.**  pet Pete
4. 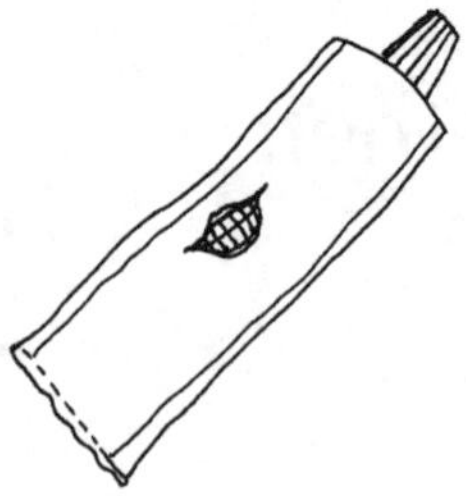 tub tube	**5.**  wet we	**6.**  rob robe
7.  cub cube	**8.** 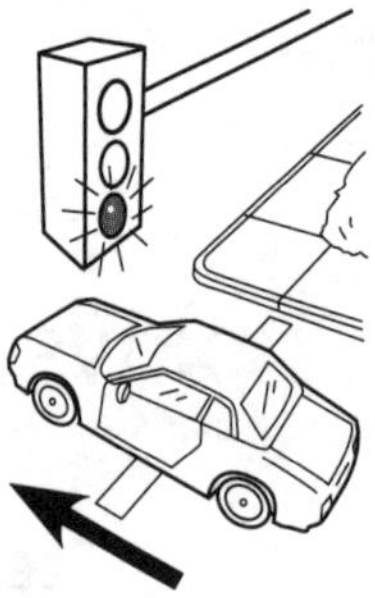 got go	**9.** 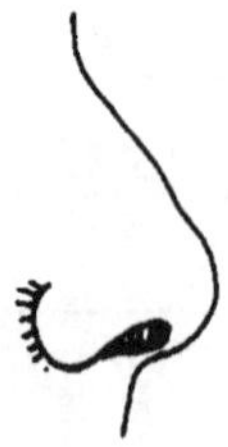 no nose

Read It Together A cute cub is not a good pet for Pete!

Name ______________________________ Date ______________

Grammar and Writing

Write Possessive Adjectives

Subject	Possessive Adjective
I	my
you	your
he	his
she	her
it	its
we	our
they	their

Look at each pair of sentences. Look at the underlined words in the first sentence. Write the correct pronoun in the second sentence.

1. I like to go exploring. I search in ________ backyard.

2. Sara and Nate came to visit. They wore ________ play clothes.

3. We crawled on the ground. It didn't matter if ________ clothes got dirty.

4. Nate wanted to see the insects. He brought ________ hand lens.

5. Sara found a caterpillar. We each looked at ________ striped back.

6. Do you like exploring, too? Next time bring ________ gear and come with us.

Name ______________________ Date ____________

Grammar

His or Her?

Grammar Rules Possessive Words

Use *her* for one girl or one woman.	Mom grows flowers in her garden.
Use *his* for one boy or one man.	Dad uses his garden tools.

Circle the correct possessive word. Write the sentence.

1. Kate writes about (his/her) pet.

Kate writes about her pet.

2. Mark tells about (his/her) frog.

3. Dad has (his/her) pen to draw.

4. Grandma is in (his/her) garden.

5. Anita reads (his/her) book.

Write a new sentence with *his* or *her*. Read it to a partner.

Name ______________________________ Date ______________

Prewrite Graphic Organizer: Story Map

Story Map

Beginning:

Middle:

End:

Organization Checklist

✓ Does the story have a beginning?
✓ Does the story have a middle?
✓ Does the story have an end?
✓ Are there words that signal the beginning, middle, and end?